CONQUERING THE SAT AND ACT EXAMS

with

Julia Ross

Julia Ross

with
Matthew Dischner

Professional Tutoring, LLC
11901 Cub Court, Fairfax Station, VA 22039   703-830-7037
info@JuliaRossPT.com   www.JuliaRossPT.com

Contents

Chapter 11 Notes

Chapter 1

Introduction to the SAT and ACT Exams

In this chapter:
• The Purpose of the SAT and ACT Exams • College Admissions Probability Organizer • Rubric for SAT/ACT Goal Essay • SAT/ACT Exam Scores Charts: Diagnostic, Practice, Goal • Registering for Your Tests: Administration Dates & Registration Guidelines • Test Day Advice

The Purpose of the SAT and ACT Exams

As the world of college admissions seems to be paradoxically growing both more streamlined and more complex, the SAT and ACT function as a major measuring point for both students and colleges/universities. Even test-optional colleges/universities use scores as one of the essential metrics of a student's college application, right behind grades and course rigor. Though perhaps not the measuring stick they were originally touted to be, these tests provide colleges with a standardized point of comparison between applicants and provide students with another opportunity to demonstrate their academic strength and capability. These tests should not be missed and should be prepared for seriously.

The SAT and ACT, however, are not the mysteries they pretend to be. With practice, guidance, studying, and a good night's sleep, students can go into these tests with confidence knowing they are putting their best selves forward.

At Professional Tutoring, we believe that competence builds confidence. Our approach to these tests is based on firsthand knowledge and has been refined over the last thirty years. With this book as a guide, our SAT/ACT prep programs prepare our students to do their best on these tests and set them off on their journey through the college admissions process with a strong, steady foot forward.

College Admissions Probability Organizer

Weighted Grade Point Average

Safety School	Safety School	Attainable School	Reach School	Reach School
- .3	- .2	Your GPA	+.2	+.3

SAT Scores

Safety School	Safety School	Attainable School	Reach School	Reach School
- 150 pts.	- 100 pts.	Reading + Math	+ 100 pts.	+ 150 pts.

ACT Scores

Safety School	Safety School	Attainable School	Reach School	Reach School
- 3 pts.	- 2 pts.	Your ACT	+ 2 pts.	+ 3 pts.

Virginia Public Universities Admission Data

Professional Tutoring, LLC - Virginia Public Universities Admission Data (Fairfax County Public School Students - Class of 2023)

No.	Name of College/University	Average Accepted SAT Score	Average Accepted ACT	Average Accepted Grade Point Average (GPA)
1	The College of William & Mary	1419	31	4.32
2	Christopher Newport University	1168	24	3.72
3	George Mason University	1218	27	3.84
4	James Madison University	1225	26	3.93
5	Longwood University	1092	22	3.49
6	Norfolk State University	935	18	3.12
7	Old Dominion University	1065	21	3.39
8	Radford University	1053	20	3.34
9	University of Mary Washington	1165	24	3.73
10	University of Virginia	1428	31	4.40
11	University of Virginia's College at Wise	1200	28	3.67
12	Virginia Commonwealth University	1183	26	3.72
13	Virginia Military Institute	1177	23	3.48
14	Virginia State University	964	17	3.14
15	Virginia Tech	1331	29	4.19

Out-of-State and Private Colleges/Universities

Professional Tutoring, LLC - Out-of-State and Private Colleges/Universities (Fairfax County Public School Students - Class of 2023)

No.	Name of College/University	Average Accepted SAT Score	Average Accepted ACT	Average Accepted Grade Point Average (GPA)
1	Amherst College	1480	34	4.07
2	Appalachian State University	1120	23	3.64
3	Auburn University	1302	28	4.03
4	Barnard College	1478	33	4.00
5	Baylor University	1268	27	4.06
6	Belmont University	1198	27	3.87
7	Binghamton University	1265	27	4.03
8	Boston College	1385	32	4.32
9	Boston University	1346	28	4.21
10	Brandeis University	1403	29	4.11
11	Brown University	1476	33	4.50
12	Bryn Mawr College	1362	31	3.94
13	Bucknell University	1313	25	4.10
14	California Institute of Technology	1539	36	4.19
15	Carnegie Mellon University	1469	34	4.40
16	Case Western Reserve University	1467	31	4.33
17	The Citadel	1069	23	3.39
18	Claremont McKenna College	1425	32	4.20
19	Clemson University	1294	26	4.12
20	College of Charleston	1172	24	3.86
21	Colorado College	1347	31	3.90

Professional Tutoring, LLC - Out-of-State and Private Colleges/Universities
(Fairfax County Public School Students - Class of 2023)

No.	Name of College/University	Average Accepted SAT Score	Average Accepted ACT	Average Accepted Grade Point Average (GPA)
22	Columbia University	1475	33	4.48
23	Cornell University	1475	32	4.44
24	Dartmouth College	1520	31	4.52
25	Davidson College	1403	31	3.80
26	DePaul University	1219	23	3.87
27	Drexel University	1306	27	3.94
28	Duke University	1530	34	4.50
29	Duquesne University	1190	26	3.76
30	East Carolina University	1089	21	3.54
31	Elon University	1217	26	3.91
32	Emory University	1481	32	4.39
33	Fairfield University	1307	29	3.70
34	Florida State University	1346	28	4.16
35	Franklin and Marshall College	1292	27	4.01
36	George Washington University	1333	30	4.16
37	Georgetown University	1478	32	4.41
38	Georgia Institute of Technology	1471	33	4.36
39	Gettysburg College	1221	23	3.85
40	Hampden-Sydney College	1097	21	3.48
41	Hampshire College	1232	26	3.79
42	Harvard University	1508	34	4.47

Professional Tutoring, LLC - Out-of-State and Private Colleges/Universities
(Fairfax County Public School Students - Class of 2023)

No.	Name of College/University	Average Accepted SAT Score	Average Accepted ACT	Average Accepted Grade Point Average (GPA)
43	Harvey Mudd College	1520	35	4.42
44	High Point University	1086	22	3.40
45	Howard University	1165	24	3.94
46	Indiana University of Pennsylvania	1049	21	3.40
47	Indiana University-Bloomington	1313	27	4.03
48	Iowa State University	1204	22	3.63
49	Johns Hopkins University	1459	31	4.40
50	Lafayette College	1389	30	4.11
51	Lehigh University	1384	29	4.19
52	Louisiana State University	1153	22	3.66
53	Marquette University	1239	23	3.86
54	Marshall University	987	14	3.17
55	Marymount University	1010	18	3.41
56	Massachusetts Institute of Technology	1540	36	4.53
57	Miami University, Oxford	1256	25	3.88
58	Michigan State University	1234	26	3.86
59	Mississippi State University	1008	20	3.33
60	Mount Holyoke College	1373	26	4.23
61	New College of Florida	1224	26	3.90
62	New York University	1435	33	4.27
63	North Carolina State University	1345	28	4.26

Professional Tutoring, LLC - Out-of-State and Private Colleges/Universities
(Fairfax County Public School Students - Class of 2023)

No.	Name of College/University	Average Accepted SAT Score	Average Accepted ACT	Average Accepted Grade Point Average (GPA)
64	Northeastern University	1381	29	4.18
65	Northwestern University	1464	32	4.42
66	Norwich University	1146	25	3.24
67	Ohio State University	1368	29	4.14
68	Ohio University	1180	23	3.75
69	Pennsylvania State University	1283	27	3.98
70	Pepperdine University	1307	29	4.23
71	Princeton University	1514	32	4.53
72	Purdue University	1417	31	4.16
73	Quinnipiac University	1000	20	3.61
74	Randolph-Macon College	1066	22	3.51
75	Rensselaer Polytechnic Institute	1453	31	4.25
76	Rice University	1492	33	4.40
77	Roanoke College	1072	24	3.43
78	Rochester Institute of Technology	1353	29	4.04
79	Rutgers University-New Brunswick	1329	30	4.04
80	Shenandoah University	1096	21	3.46
81	Smith College	1516	34	4.30
82	Southern Methodist University	1415	32	3.70
83	Stanford University	1505	35	4.54
84	Stony Brook University	1357	30	4.01
85	Syracuse University	1290	27	4.08
86	Texas A & M University	1322	30	4.01

Professional Tutoring, LLC - Out-of-State and Private Colleges/Universities
(Fairfax County Public School Students - Class of 2023)

No.	Name of College/University	Average Accepted SAT Score	Average Accepted ACT	Average Accepted Grade Point Average (GPA)
87	Texas Christian University	1235	28	4.03
88	Tulane University of Louisiana	1303	31	4.14
89	U.S. Air Force Academy	1363	27	4.25
90	U.S. Coast Guard Academy	1316	28	4.24
91	U.S. Merchant Marine Academy	1326	28	3.99
92	U.S. Military Academy	1370	27	4.08
93	U.S. Naval Academy	1356	28	4.22
94	University at Buffalo (SUNY)	1304	28	3.87
95	University of Alabama	1229	25	3.81
96	University of Alabama at Birmingham	1247	25	3.80
97	University of Arizona	1188	23	3.61
98	University of California-Berkeley	1419	34	4.35
99	University of California-Davis	1422	31	4.25
100	University of California-Irvine	1405	31	4.30
101	University of California-Los Angeles	1489	35	4.42
102	University of California-San Diego	1477	32	4.41
103	University of California-Santa Barbara	1429	30	4.31
104	University of Chicago	1476	32	4.31
105	University of Colorado Boulder	1326	29	4.03
106	University of Connecticut	1338	28	4.09
107	University of Delaware	1255	27	4.03

Professional Tutoring, LLC - Out-of-State and Private Colleges/Universities
(Fairfax County Public School Students - Class of 2023)

No.	Name of College/University	Average Accepted SAT Score	Average Accepted ACT	Average Accepted Grade Point Average (GPA)
108	University of Florida	1411	30	4.27
109	University of Georgia	1362	28	4.27
110	University of Illinois at Urbana-Champaign	1489	32	4.35
111	University of Iowa	1256	25	4.07
112	University of Kansas	1186	25	3.59
113	University of Kentucky	1150	22	3.54
114	University of Lynchburg	1070	15	3.20
115	University of Mary Washington	1165	24	3.73
116	University of Maryland-College Park	1434	31	4.30
117	University of Massachusetts-Amherst	1345	28	4.14
118	University of Miami	1329	27	4.16
119	University of Michigan-Ann Arbor	1488	33	4.39
120	University of Minnesota-Twin Cities	1349	27	4.10
121	University of Mississippi	1095	21	3.50
122	University of Missouri-Columbia	1239	27	3.75
123	University of Missouri-Kansas City	1340	25	3.50
124	University of Nebraska-Lincoln	1186	26	3.74
125	University of New Hampshire	1237	26	3.92
126	University of North Carolina at Chapel Hill	1491	32	4.43
127	University of North Carolina at Charlotte	1158	24	3.87

Professional Tutoring, LLC - Out-of-State and Private Colleges/Universities
(Fairfax County Public School Students - Class of 2023)

No.	Name of College/University	Average Accepted SAT Score	Average Accepted ACT	Average Accepted Grade Point Average (GPA)
128	University of Notre Dame	1459	31	4.40
129	University of Oregon	1237	26	3.79
130	University of Pennsylvania	1495	31	4.50
131	University of Pittsburgh	1378	30	4.13
132	University of Rhode Island	1197	24	3.84
133	University of Richmond	1321	29	4.29
134	University of Rochester	1397	31	4.27
135	University of South Carolina-Columbia	1273	26	4.14
136	University of Southern California	1385	31	4.26
137	University of Tennessee-Chattanooga	1133	23	3.60
138	University of Tennessee-Knoxville	1271	26	4.01
139	University of Texas at Austin	1374	31	4.26
140	University of Vermont	1300	29	4.04
141	University of Washington-Seattle Campus	1404	30	4.29
142	University of Wisconsin-Madison	1408	30	4.27
143	Vanderbilt University	1447	31	4.31
144	Vassar College	1465	33	4.37
145	Wake Forest University	1373	31	4.27
146	Washington University in St Louis	1419	31	4.45
147	Wellesley College	1416	35	4.34
148	West Virginia University	1114	22	3.53
149	William & Mary	1419	31	4.32
150	Yale University	1506	33	4.52

SAT/ACT Goal Score Essay

You will each prepare a five-paragraph essay for me detailing your college and SAT/ACT exam goals. Goal setting and visualization play a critical role in success. Take time to sit down with your parents and discuss your future. Use the following format. Impress us! ☺

1ˢᵗ Paragraph: In this paragraph, you will write about your family and background. Tell me where you grew up, how many members are in your family, and your interests.

2ⁿᵈ Paragraph: In this paragraph, you will write about your schooling and academic experience up to now (your junior/senior year). Begin with a sketch of your primary school years (1ˢᵗ – 6ᵗʰ grades) and then your middle and upper school years. Have you enjoyed school? What parts do you like best? Tell me about the classes that you found most interesting. What have you found most interesting/easiest/most difficult? Do you participate in extracurricular activities?

3ʳᵈ Paragraph: What do you plan to do after high school? Will you immediately enroll in a four-year college/university? Do you have a dream school? What majors are you considering? What do you want to do as an adult?

4ᵗʰ Paragraph: Please analyze the SAT and ACT exams that you took in the beginning of the course. Do you notice any patterns? Was one section easier for you than the others? Did you finish each section? Did you omit lots of questions, a few, or none? What did you do well? What did not go so well?

5ᵗʰ Paragraph: Now it is time to set your goals for the two sections of the SAT exam and the four sections of the ACT. As we discussed in class, you will base your goals on several criteria:

1. Your College Dreams;

2. Your GPA;

3. Your work ethic and time commitment to studying for this class; and

4. Discussion with your parents.

SAT DIAGNOSTIC SCORE:

Reading/Writing: _____   Math: _____   Total: _____

SAT GOAL SCORE:

Reading/Writing: _____   Math: _____   Total: _____

ACT DIAGNOSTIC SCORE:

English: _____   Math: _____   Reading: _____

Science: _____   Total: _____

Optional Essay (Writing): _____

ACT GOAL SCORE:

English: _____   Math: _____   Reading: _____

Science: _____   Total: _____

Optional Essay (Writing): _____

SAT Goals and Scores Sheet

Name: _____ Class Session: _____ P.T. ID#: _____

Test	Date Taken	Reading & Writing	Math	Total	Change
Diagnostic CB Test #_____					
SAT Goal Score					
PSAT - 10th Grade					
PSAT - 11th Grade					
SAT Practice Test# _____					
SAT Practice Test# _____					
SAT Practice Test# _____					
SAT Practice Test# _____					
Best Scores					
SAT Exam #1					
SAT Exam #2					

The ACT Goals and Scores Sheet

Name: _____ Class Session: _____ P.T. ID#: _____

Test	Date	English	Math	Rdg	Science	Writing	Comp. Score	Change
Diagnostic ACT # _____								
ACT Goal Score								
Practice Test ACT# _____								
Practice Test ACT# _____								
Practice Test ACT# _____								
Practice Test ACT# _____								
Best Scores								
ACT Test #1								
ACT Test #2								

Registering for Your Tests

Approximate SAT Administration Dates & Registration Deadlines

* Dates do change each year. The dates indicated here are approximate dates to help you plan only. You must verify dates at CollegeBoard.com!

Test Dates	Registration Deadline	Late Registration
August	July 25	August 15
October	September 1	September 15
November	October 1	October 15
December	November 1	November 15
March	February 1	February 15
May	April 1	April 15
June	May 1	May 15

Registration:

For Juniors: Register by **February 1st** for the May **and** the June exams. Register for your base school or another local school.

For Seniors: Register by **July 1st** for the two of the following three exam dates: August, October **and** November exams. Register for your base school or another local school.

Website: www.CollegeBoard.org

SAT Registration Guidelines

SAT Exam:

Sophomores and **Juniors:** The Professional Tutoring SAT/ACT Preparation nine-month and six-month courses prepare 10th and 11th graders for the SAT Exam, which satisfies college/university admission test requirements. This is a two-hour test. The test must be taken as a whole; students cannot take a subset of the test. This SAT/ACT Preparation Course prepares students to take the SAT exam two times (May and June). In general, students achieve their highest score after finishing the class. There is no limit to the number of times that one may sit for the SAT, but most students take it two to three times.

Seniors: This class prepares rising 12th graders for the SAT Exam, which satisfies college/university admission test requirements. This is a two-hour test. The test must be taken as a whole; students cannot take a subset of the test. There is no limit to the number of times that one may sit for the SAT, however most students take it two to three times. This SAT Preparation Course prepares students to take the exam two times during their senior year (August, October and/or November). In general, students achieve their highest score after finishing the class.

Exam Dates:

The SAT is offered seven times throughout the year.

Registration:

Students may register for the SAT online at www.collegeboard.org. It is best to register for the exams as early as possible to ensure a space **at your base school exam center**. Make sure to write down your College Board username and password for future reference; you will need these repeatedly in the upcoming months!

ID Requirements:

Students are required to show a photo ID to take the exam. The photo ID must have a clear photograph that matches the test-taker and must be one that is government-issued (i.e. driver's license, passport, or military ID) or ID from the school you currently attend or the notarized *College Board Student ID Form* (available from school counselor and prepared by your school). Acceptable ID must be original, valid, current, and have your full name exactly as it appears on the Admission Ticket.

Photo Submission:

The College Board requires a digital submission of an identifying photograph at registration. This photograph will become part of the student's test registration and Admission Ticket and will be compared to the student's approved photo ID at the test site.

Photo requirements:
- Submit during online registration

- Photograph, preferably digital and not copy
- Clear and in focus with good lighting, full face view, only head and shoulders
- Digital specs: Minimum of 325 X 390 pixels, formatted in .jpg or .gif or .png.
- Religious head coverings must match photo ID and in-person at the test site

Test Day Entrance: In-person appearance MUST match the photo. Students must have both the photo admission ticket <u>and</u> an acceptable form of photo ID for entry to the test center and upon entry to the test room.

Scores: Students may view their scores approximately two weeks after completing the exam (www.collegeboard.org – user name and password required). We recommend that Professional Tutoring SAT Preparation students take the SAT Exam only two times during the course (May and June for juniors, and two times during the fall August, October, November. Most students will achieve their highest scores in these short periods.

Accommodations: Students who have a current Individualized Education Plan, a 504 Plan, or other in-school accommodations may be eligible for testing accommodations, such as additional testing time, or a reader. If you are eligible for accommodations and have not yet begun to work with the College Board to set them up, see me!

Certifications: Test proctors will be able to compare the picture on the Admission Ticket to both the student's photo ID and the student's face. Test takers will also be required to sign a certification statement regarding accuracy of all submissions, complicity to testing security, and acknowledgment of law enforcement issues for engaging in impersonation.

Caveats: Students are responsible for understanding and following the SAT identification requirements and policies. Any questions should be addressed to Customer Service at the College Board well in advance of test day. It is your responsibility to ensure that your ID documents are up-to-date and available on the day of the test. Questionable ID is subject to College Board review and approval before, during, or after the test administration.

Approximate ACT Administration Dates & Registration Deadlines

* Dates can change each year. The dates indicated here are cautious planning dates. Verify dates at ACT.org.

Test Dates	Registration Deadline	Late Registration
September	August 1	August 15
October	September 15	October 1
December	November 1	November 15
February	January 15	February 1
April	March 1	March 15
June	May 1	May 15
July	June 15	July 1

Registration:

For Juniors: Register by **February 1st** for the April **and** the June exams. Register for your base school or another local school.

For Seniors: Register by **August 1st** for the September **and** October exams. Register for your base school or another local school.

Website: www.ACT.org

ACT Registration Guidelines

The ACT Test:

Sophomores and Juniors: The Professional Tutoring SAT/ACT Preparation nine-month and six-month courses prepare 10th and 11th graders for the ACT Test, which satisfies college/university admission test requirements. This is a 2-hour and 55-minute test with an optional 40-minute writing (essay) section. Excluding the writing section, the test must be taken as a whole; students cannot take a subset of the test. Students are permitted to take the ACT up to twelve times, however, most students take it between 2-3 times. This SAT/ACT Preparation Course prepares students to take the ACT exam two times (April and June). In general, students achieve their highest score after finishing the class.

Seniors: This class prepares rising 12th graders for the ACT Test, which satisfies college/university admission test requirements. This is a 2-hour 55-minute test with an optional 40-minute writing section. Excluding the writing section, the test must be taken as a whole; students cannot take a subset of the test. Students are permitted to take the ACT up to twelve times, however, most students take it between 2-3 times. This SAT/ACT Preparation Course prepares students to take each exam two times during their senior year (September and October). In general, students achieve their highest score after finishing the class.

Exam Dates:

The ACT is offered seven times during the year.

Registration:

Students may register for the ACT Test online at www.act.org. It is best to register for the exams as early as possible to ensure a space **at your base school exam center**. Make sure to write down your ACT username and password for future reference; you will need these repeatedly in the upcoming months!

ID Requirements:

Students are required to show a photo ID to take the exam. The photo ID must have a clear photograph that matches the test-taker and must be one that is government-issued (i.e. driver's license, passport, or military ID) or ID from the school you currently attend or the notarized *ACT Student Identification Form* (available from the school counselor and prepared by the school). Acceptable ID must be original, valid, and current, and have the student's name exactly as it appears on the ACT admissions ticket.

Photo Submission:

The ACT requires a digital submission of an identifying photograph at registration. This photograph will become part of the student's test registration and admissions ticket and will be compared to the student's approved photo ID at the test site.

Photo requirements:
- Preferably digital and not copy
- Clear and in focus with good lighting, full face view, only head and shoulders, against a plain background
- Digital specs: Minimum of 640 X 480 pixels, formatted in .jpg, .jpeg, .png, or .bmp
- Photo must be uploaded <u>at least</u> 8 days prior to test date
- Religious head-coverings must match photo and in-person at test site

Test Day Entrance: In-person appearance MUST match your photos. Students must have both the photo admission ticket <u>and</u> an acceptable form of photo ID for entry to the test center and upon entry to the test room and for the collection of answer sheets.

Scores: Students may view their scores within two weeks of completing the exam (www.act.org – username and password required). We recommend that Professional Tutoring SAT/ACT Preparation students take the ACT Test only two times during the course (April and June). Most students will achieve their highest scores in this short period.

Accommodations: Students who have a current Individualized Education Plan, a 504 Plan, or who have testing accommodations at school may be eligible for testing accommodations, such as additional testing time, bubbling support, or a reader. If you are eligible for accommodations and have not yet begun to work with the ACT to set them up, make sure to see a Professional Tutoring staff member or your high school counselor.

Certifications: Test proctors will be able to compare the picture on the Admission Ticket to both the student's photo ID and the student's face. Test takers will also be required to sign a certification statement on the ACT answer sheet regarding the accuracy of all submissions, complicity to testing security, and acknowledgment of law enforcement issues for engaging in impersonation.

Caveats: Students are responsible for understanding and following the ACT identification requirements and policies. Any questions should be addressed to Customer Service at the ACT well in advance of test day. It is your responsibility to ensure that your ID documents are up-to-date and available on the day of the test. Questionable ID is subject to ACT review and approval before, during, or after the test administration.

Test Day Advice

Over three decades of preparing students to take the SAT and ACT exams, Professional Tutoring has developed a list of test day tips. Seriously, some of these tips may seem silly to you BUT...they can make or break your SAT/ACT exam! Trust me; I am old with lots of experience in helping students through this process.

1. Register to take the SAT/ACT Exams at your local school, if offered. You will feel much more comfortable in your own environment.

2. If you are not able to register for your base school, have your parents plan on driving you to the test center. When a student gets lost or has trouble finding a parking spot, they will enter the test feeling stressed. This is not a good way to begin these critically important exams.

3. At least one week before the exam administration, CHECK your entrance ticket carefully to make sure that you are registered for the correct test at the correct location, and that you have the correct identification. Leave nothing to chance.

4. Students should drive <u>with their parents or alone</u> to the test site. It is important to remain focused in the time leading to the exam.

5. Make sure that everything is ready in a backpack/bag the night before the exam: driver's license, test admissions form, laptop with Bluebook app installed (for the SAT), calculator and extra batteries (for the ACT), pencils, snack/lunch, change for the vending machines, and gas in the car.

6. Rest the night before the exam—no cramming, no sleepovers and no partying!

7. Eat a "normal" breakfast. Do not overdo or underdo this meal.

8. You may bring water to the test center.

9. Install the Bluebook testing app on your laptop and try it out ahead of time! Try the practice questions and take the practice exams so you are comfortable using the app on test day. You do not want to be learning a new app interface on test day!

10. TEST DAY EMERGENCIES: While some emergencies are fixable, many of the following situations simply mean that you will need to take the test another time. These are just some of the many reasons that we recommend registering for multiple, consecutive testing dates. All of these have happened to our students at some point, so be aware and take all the precautions you can!

    - Wrong test center: ALWAYS double-check the address on your ticket before test day. If you go to the wrong test center and cannot get to the correct one before 8 AM, you cannot take the exam.

    - No Identification: Neither the SAT nor the ACT will let you into the exam without proper identification. If you are not able to somehow obtain your identification in time to take the test, you will have to take the test at another time.

- No Laptop: While testing centers are supposed to have backup laptops for students to use for the SAT, these are likely to be a limited supply and of questionable reliability. Make sure your laptop is packed along with its charger. Charge the laptop and install the Bluebook app ahead of time!

- No Calculator: While forgetting your calculator will not prevent you from taking theACT (it is possible to solve all of the questions without a calculator), it will prevent you from doing your best. Extra calculators will not be available at the testing center, so pack your calculator and extra batteries for it in your bag the night before.

- Misbubbling: This mistake is often fixable, especially if you catch it right away. If you notice that you have begun to misbubble, immediately notify your proctor. If you only realize your mistake after you have completed the test or after receiving your score report, you may still be able to salvage your score by submitting a request for score verification. If the mistake is obvious, they should be able to correct it and update your score accordingly.

- Sickness: This is one of the more common "emergencies," and unfortunately there is no helping it. If you do decide to take the exam while you are sick, you will most likely not get your best score. You are usually better off waiting until the next testing date.

Reassurance!

Everyone should remember that the students will have completed an extensive SAT/ACT preparation course. You have done a great job studying and are so much more prepared than you were several months ago and so much more ready than almost everyone else!

Chapter 2

Preparing and Strategizing for the Exams

In this chapter:

- What Is the SAT Exam?
- SAT Exam Overview
- What is the ACT Exam?
- ACT Exam Overview
- Strategies for Taking the Exams
- Guidelines for Studying for Your SAT/ACT Exams
- SAT vs. ACT Scoring Comparison: Concordance Table

What Is the SAT Exam?

SAT Exam

- Knowledge and reasoning-based exam

- 2-hour and 14-minute exam with two Multiple Choice Sections (each divided into two modules), a total of 98 questions

- The test is digital and taken through the Bluebook App on a laptop. A calculator and other tools are built into the app, though students can bring their own calculator if they choose.

- The test is adaptive and alters based on student success in the first module (early questions).

- 2 sub-scores (Reading/Writing and Math), each worth between 200 and 800 points.

- The maximum total score is 1600, the sum of the two sub-scores.

- $60 registration fee

- Saturday exam days

When Should I Take the SAT Exam?

- Exams are offered seven times each year:

  August, October, November, December, March, May, and June

- Professional Tutoring recommends that juniors take the May & June SAT Exams and that seniors take the August & October SAT Exams or October and November Exams.

- **www.CollegeBoard.com**

SAT Exam Overview

The SAT tests critical reading, writing, and math skills. The following will give you a general overview of the test and some basic strategies to help you gain confidence in attaining a better score.

SAT Exam Format

The SAT Exam is 2 hours and 14 minutes long with a ten-minute break in the middle. The exam is mostly made up of multiple-choice questions and is divided into the following sections:

	Section	Length	Content	Type	# of Questions
1.	Reading and Writing Module 1	32 Minutes	Reading comprehension, vocabulary in context, grammar, and editing skills	Multiple Choice	27
2.	Reading and Writing Module2	35 Minutes	Same as above	Multiple Choice	27
3.	Math Module 1	35 Minutes	High school algebra and geometry, numbers and operations, statistics, probability and data analysis	Multiple Choice and Free Response	22
4.	Math module 2	35 Minutes	Same as above	Multiple Choice and Free Response	32

Scoring

1. You receive points for correct answers, with difficult questions weighted to give more points.

2. Depending on performance in the first module of each section, students will either receive an easier or harder second module, worth fewer or more total points respectively.

3. While you do not lose any points for incorrect answers or questions left blank, you ONLY earn points for correct answers to do your best to answer every question well!

4. Each section (Reading/Writing and Math) is worth between 200 and 800 points, and the total maximum score for the entire SAT exam is 1600 points.

5. Because the test is weighted and adaptive, success in early questions can impact the total maximum available score. A student who receives the "easier" second modules for both sections can score a maximum of 1400 points. A student who receives "harder" second modules for both sections can score a maximum of 1600 points.

What Is the ACT Exam?

ACT Exam

- Achievement test that is knowledge and curriculum-based

- Measures high school achievement

- 2-hour 55-minute exam with 215 multiple choice questions

- Made up of 4 sections each worth up to 36 points:

English   Math   Reading   Science

- Optional 40-minute Writing Section (essay) available

- Composite score is the average of the four sections, Maximum composite score is 36

- Writing section scored from 2-12

- $52 registration fee or $68 fee with Writing Section

- Saturday exam days

When Should I take the ACT Exam?

- ACT Exams are offered seven times throughout the year:

  September, October, December, February, April, June, and July

- April & June ACT exams for junior year recommended

- September & October ACT exams for senior year recommended

www.ACT.org

ACT Exam Overview

The ACT tests English, math, reading, and science. The following will give you a general overview of the test and some basic strategies to help you gain confidence in earning the best score that you can.

ACT Format

The ACT is 2 hours and 55 minutes long with a ten-minute break in between the math and reading tests. If you choose to take the writing test, you will also get a five-minute break after the science test. The exam includes only multiple-choice questions and is divided into the following sections:

	Section	Length	Content	Type	# of Questions
1.	English Test	45 Minutes	Grammar, vocabulary in context, and editing skills	Multiple Choice	75
2.	Math Test	60 Minutes	HS geometry and algebra, numbers and operations, statistics, probability and data analysis	Multiple Choice	60
3.	Reading Test	35 Minutes	Reading Comprehension	Multiple Choice	40
4.	Science Test	35 Minutes	General scientific knowledge, data analysis, experimental design	Multiple Choice	40
5.	Writing Test (optional)	40 Minutes	Analyze and compare different perspectives on an issue	Essay	1

ACT Scoring

1. You gain one point for each correct answer on the ACT. This raw score is then converted to a scaled score of 1-36.

2. Each section (English, Math, Reading, and Science) is scored from 1-36 points, and the composite score for the entire ACT test is the average of those four scores. The optional Essay section is scored out of a possible 12 points.

Rules for Taking the Exams

1. You cannot jump back and forth between timed sections.

2. You cannot return to earlier sections to change your answers.

3. You cannot spend any additional time in a section once your time is up.

4. You can move around within a section as much as you want.

5. You can look ahead within a section to see (or preview) what kinds of questions are coming.

Strategies for Taking the Exams

1. Directions never change, you will have them all memorized by the end of this course. SO DON'T WASTE TIME READING THEM.

2. Make an educated guess rather than leaving a question blank. You don't lose any points for guessing on the SAT or ACT.

3. Answer ALL free response questions on the SAT. You have nothing to lose.

4. Check your answer sheet once in a while to make sure your answers and questions are lined up.

5. Mark The questions you decide to answer later so they are easy to find.

6. Wear a non-smart watch and keep track of the time—especially when reading long passages.

7. Read the question carefully before you look at the answer choices.

8. Try to make up your own answer (prediction) before you even look at the answer choices.

9. Find a couple of quick points if you are running out of time, especially if you are working on reading comprehension.

Guidelines for Studying for Your SAT and ACT Exams

Weekly Review:

1. Attend class and pay attention. Do not sit near a friend or other distraction. Make sure that you sit where you can see the whiteboard well. I see lots of squinting.

2. Make sure to ask questions in class. It is crucial that you direct questions to your instructors. They cannot differentiate between chatting and "working" with another student.

3. Complete your homework carefully. Check all the answers in the back of the workbook, vocabulary book, and test book.

4. Form a study group of two to three students. Commit and meet weekly! See below for study group ideas.

Reading and Writing Review:

1. Review vocabulary (current and old lists) 4-5 times per week for 15-20 minutes per session. This is crucial to your success in the Reading And Writing sections. Prepare for vocabulary quizzes.

2. Parents, please review the lists and try to use these words in your daily household conversations. One pitfall is that students use the literal meaning (denotation) of a new word and miss its connotation. Students often need help remembering pronunciation; this helps the kids remember the words and recognize them in reading and conversation.

3. Read for pleasure!! Some good books include *The Hot Zone*, the *Harry Potter* series, *Jane Eyre*, etc.

4. Re-read the initial assignments in the syllabus.

5. Review the Reading Overview in Chapter Three.

6. Review the Writing Overview and worksheets in Chapter Three.

Math Review:

Go over the practice math exercises included in this book, especially any lessons you found difficult in class. Re-do problems until you understand! Prepare for math quizzes.

Testing Review:

Students may review the tests that they are not going to be working on in class. It is a really good idea to work on practice problems.

Form a Study Group:

It is important to set up study groups. While the kids should be mature enough to do this on their own, this is usually not the case. The setup and initial sessions require consistent parental involvement. My recommendations for study groups are:

1. Students may review ONLY the tests not listed on their syllabus. It is a really good idea to work on practice problems.

2. Choose a group of 2-3 students for a study group (parents and students should do this collaboratively).

3. Students should make contact with their chosen study group. If they do not do so within a specified time period as agreed at home, parents should contact parents.

4. Study groups should plan on 2-hour sessions once or twice per week.

5. In the study group, students should do the following:

   – Homework

   – Vocabulary review (current and old words)

   – Practice SAT/ACT questions

6. Parents should help facilitate the meeting by remaining in the study room for the entire two-hour period for at least the first 4-6 sessions. Parents can help by making vocabulary flashcards, quizzing on the vocabulary words, and working out any reading/math/writing problems.

7. Set up a specific study group time that does NOT vary EVER. Even if only one student can make the study group, go ahead and have it. Once changes begin, it is really hard to get back on track.

8. Feeding the kids does work wonders too!

SAT vs. ACT Scoring Comparison: Concordance Table

SAT Total (400-1600)	ACT Composite Score	SAT Total (400-1600)	ACT Composite Score	SAT Total (400-1600)	ACT Composite Score
1600	36	1250	26	900	16
1590	36	1240	26	890	16
1580	36	1230	26	880	16
1570	36	1220	25	870	15
1560	35	1210	25	860	15
1550	35	1200	25	850	15
1540	35	1190	24	840	15
1530	35	1180	24	830	15
1520	34	1170	24	820	14
1510	34	1160	24	810	14
1500	34	1150	23	800	14
1490	34	1140	23	790	14
1480	33	1130	23	780	14
1470	33	1120	22	770	13
1460	33	1110	22	760	13
1450	33	1100	22	750	13
1440	32	1090	21	740	13
1430	32	1080	21	730	13
1420	32	1070	21	720	12
1410	31	1060	21	710	12
1400	31	1050	20	700	12
1390	31	1040	20	690	12
1380	30	1030	20	680	11
1370	30	1020	19	670	11
1360	30	1010	19	660	11
1350	29	1000	19	650	11
1340	29	990	19	640	10
1330	29	980	18	630	10
1320	28	970	18	620	10
1310	28	960	18	610	9
1300	28	950	17	600	9
1290	27	940	17	590	9
1280	27	930	17	580	8
1270	27	920	17	570	8
1260	27	910	16	560	8

Chapter 3

The Language Arts: Reading and Writing

In this chapter:
<ul><li>Reading and Writing Overview</li><li>The SAT Reading and Writing Section</li><li>The ACT English Test</li><li>The ACT Reading Test</li><li>General Language Arts Tips</li></ul>

Reading and Writing Overview

Both the SAT and the ACT devote half of their respective exams to testing language arts skills: reading and writing. These sections test not just your ability to read and understand a text, but, also, your ability to analyze and, if necessary, correctly rearrange it. These sections test your vocabulary, your knowledge of grammar, and your command of the English language.

However, the SAT and ACT differ significantly in how they test this knowledge. On the SAT's Reading and Writing section, reading comprehension, analysis, language, and grammar are mixed together. Each multiple-choice question presents an approximately paragraph-long passage and then asks a question about the passage. Each question stands alone: the reading presented in one question will not be used for the next.

On the ACT, the language arts questions are divided into two separate sections: English, which primarily tests grammar and knowledge of the English language, and Reading, which primarily tests reading comprehension. Both of these sections are passage-based: students are presented with a passage and then 10-15 questions about that passage.

Despite these structural differences, students will find much in common between the two tests, and preparing for both side-by-side will definitely strengthen their language arts skills. In preparing for these tests, students will find that both the SAT and ACT Exams cover similar categories of passages on the following topics:

- Prose Fiction/Literary Narrative

- History/Humanities

- Social Science

- Natural Science

A strong vocabulary is of the utmost importance in preparing for the language arts sections of both the SAT and ACT. Vocabulary preparation is a tedious part of SAT/ACT preparation. Studying vocabulary is like doing sit-ups. It can be boring and somewhat painful, but pays off in core strengthening. Reviewing vocabulary will strengthen your core SAT/ACT knowledge. Both tests focus on "high-utility academic words and phrases," or "Tier Two" vocabulary. Tier Two words appear in many different texts across different domains, and they often have multiple meanings, which makes understanding the context in which they are used of great importance.

Despite what many students might wish, there is no good way to prepare for the language arts portions of these tests without reading. Reading comprehension is a skill learned over time, and while short-term studying and practice can help, there is no substitute for actually sitting down with a book. Good preparation will include **reading for pleasure** on your own – it is the best vocabulary tool. Some books that might interest you are:

1. *The Hot Zone* by Richard Preston

2. The *Harry Potter* Series by J.K. Rowling

3. The *Hunger Games* Series by Suzanne Collins

4. *Great Expectations* by Charles Dickens

5. *The House of the Spirits* by Isabelle Allende

You should also make sure you are reading (and we mean actually reading, not Sparknoting!) the books you are assigned in your English classes. Reading for a class is not necessarily fun, but you would be surprised how often these tests use texts or writers you are exposed to in school. Here are some general strategies for answering different types of Reading questions.

1. Take the SAT and ACT Exams seriously. They are designed to test students' reasoning and knowledge skills so make sure that you think through every question.

2. Use a process of elimination. Look at all four of the multiple-choice answers. Do not pick one until you have considered ALL four.

3. Consider each answer carefully.

4. Make a dot next to the possible correct answers and strike through the obviously incorrect answers.

5. Whittle down the answers to pick the correct one.

6. Remember that any answer you choose should be substantiated (proven true) by evidence from the passage. If you are unsure of an answer, do not just guess from memory—look for the answer in the passage.

7. If you are having trouble, some questions ask for proof, with specific lines cited. Go to those lines, brainstorm what point they prove, and try to match it with one of the given answers.

8. Remember, though multiple answer choices in a question may be factually true or grammatically correct, only one choice actually answers the question you are being asked. Look for keywords or specifics in the question itself to make sure you are actually addressing what it asks!

The SAT Reading and Writing Section

The SAT Reading and Writing test is divided into two modules, each with 32 minutes to complete 27 multiple-choice questions. Each question is paired with an individual passage; passages do not carry over from question to question. The type and length of these passages can vary significantly. You will see literature, poetry, history, social sciences, humanities, and the natural sciences, and the texts will often vary from 25 to 150 words. The SAT categorizes its reading and writing section questions in four ways:

1. **Information and Ideas**: These questions are your general reading comprehension questions. The test is checking if you properly understood the text, or possibly that you are correctly interpreting a table or a graph.

2. **Craft and Structure**: These questions require the student to analyze the way in which the text is written. They can involve choosing the correct vocabulary, rearranging sentences to make sure the text flows logically, or finding the connections between two related texts.

3. **Expression of Ideas**: Most of these questions involve editing or improving a text, not simply correcting an error. The student often has to identify what goal the text was trying to accomplish and revise the text so that it achieves that goal.

4. **Standard English Conventions**: These are your typical grammar questions. They often require students to fix some grammatical mistakes. These can vary from verb tense and agreement questions to questions about proper punctuation.

As discussed in Chapter 2, the entire SAT is adaptive. The SAT Reading and Writing section is divided into two modules, and performance on the first module affects which modules you receive for the second. The SAT rates questions into three difficulty categories, with the most difficult questions worth more points. The difficulty of the first module is always evenly balanced, but students who do well on the first module will receive a harder second module. However, while harder, this second module is worth more points, and it is necessary if a student wants to score above 700.

While easier said than done, we strongly suggest students do their best not to obsess too much about the difficulty rating of the questions. Question difficulty in the reading section is often student-dependent; a hard text for one student is an easy text for another based on their background and reading experiences. It sounds cliche, but simply do your best on each question, regardless of whether you think it is an "easy" or "difficult" question.

Common Types of SAT Reading and Writing Questions:

1. **Overall Meaning/Purpose**: These questions will focus on the main idea of the passage. You may be asked to look at "the big picture" and ignore smaller details.

2. **Meaning in Context**: These questions will focus on a specific idea in the passage and ask for an explanation or inference.

3. **Interpretation**: These questions may ask, "Why does the author say…?', or, "What does the author mean by…". Students must answer based on reasoning or evidence. Make sure to look at the author's choice of words, tone, and specific details supplied in the passage.

4. **Tone/Mood**: These questions will ask "How does the author feel about…?" Look for specific vocabulary and connotations to help answer these questions.

5. **Synthesis**: These questions will ask how ideas relate to each other in the passage. It sometimes involves reading a bulleted list of information and then picking out specifics to accomplish a certain goal.

6. **Vocabulary in Context:** These questions will ask about the denotations or connotations of vocabulary found in the passage. Sometimes, these questions are presented as "fill-in-the-blank" vocabulary questions. Remember, many words have more than one meaning; you must identify the meaning appropriate to the passage.

7. **Identifying Sentence Errors**: These questions cover grammar, sentence structure, word choice, and idiomatic expressions. The passage will have underlined sentence parts; each sentence part will include one or more words. You will need to spot the error if there is one. More grammar and punctuation rules are covered at the end of the chapter.

8. **Improving Phrases**: When an entire sentence (or phrase within a sentence) is underlined, students will often need to rearrange or reword the underlined section in order to make sure it is grammatically correct and makes sense within the passage.

The ACT English Test

The ACT English test is 45 minutes long, with 75 questions divided equally between five passages. Students are tested on their command of the English language and their knowledge of the "Conventions of Standard English". Generally, this means questions cover grammar, sentence structure, and vocabulary. You will also find questions relating to overall sequencing and content. The types of passages used by the ACT do not follow a set pattern, but are generally nonfiction, ranging from journalistic pieces to history to narrative scientific reports.

The ACT categorizes its English test questions in the following three ways:

1. **Conventions of Standard English**: People traditionally associate the English section with these questions. These primarily focus on punctuation, grammar, and sentence structure. These are usually presented with a word, phrase, punctuation mark, or some combination underlined within the text. The student is then asked to, if necessary, correct the underlined portion.

2. **Production of Writing**: These questions focus on structure, sequencing, and author intent. They may involve deciding whether or not to include an additional sentence in a paragraph, or reordering parts of the text in order to make sure information flows logically. As well, though less common, these questions may require students to analyze the author's intent in their writing.

3. **Knowledge of Language**: These questions analyze word choice. They often require the student to look at both denotation and connotation, the literal meaning of a word as well as its figurative association or tone.

When going through the ACT English section, we suggest taking things paragraph by paragraph. By reading each passage one paragraph at a time and answering questions focusing on the single paragraph, you will find that you do not get bored or lose focus and forget what you have just read. It will also help you to more accurately answer questions that rely on context clues.

Multiple Choice Questions on the ACT English Test

The multiple-choice writing questions will focus on the mechanics of writing, including:

1. Identifying Sentence Errors (grammar, usage, style questions).

2. Improving Sentences

3. Improving Paragraphs

Identifying Sentence Errors:

These types of questions cover grammar, sentence structure, word choice, and idiomatic expressions. The ACT will provide passages with underlined sentence parts; each sentence part will include one or more words. Each underlined portion will correspond to a question number. The first answer choice of the question will usually give the "no change" option, and the next three answer choices will give options for potential corrections. You will need to spot the error if there is one. Approximately one out of every four questions will have no error. Remember that all sentences must have a subject and a verb and express a complete thought. More grammar and punctuation rules are covered at the end of the chapter.

Strategies to Identify Sentence Errors:

1. Read the whole sentence; listen for the mistake.

2. If the mistake is clear to you, choose the answer that fixes it. Make sure to glance at all the answers, as always.

3. If the mistake is not clear, read each underlined choice again and eliminate the choices that contain errors.

4. Make a final choice.

5. Check your final answer in the sentence.

Improving Sentences:

Improving Sentence questions will focus on the structure of entire sentences. In this type of question, the test will underline an awkward phrase. There will be four possible answers, and the first will usually be "no change". The other options may or may not be better than the underlined phrase.

Strategies:

1. Read the whole sentence.

2. Think about the underlined phrase. Decide if it is correct.

3. In most cases, predict a good improvement.

4. Consider each of the answer choices.

5. Use the process of elimination.

6. Check your final answer in the sentence.

Improving Paragraphs:

The Improving Paragraph questions focus on improving sentence structure, word choice, and organization of the paragraph. Many times, questions will ask you to re-order the sentences to make the entire paragraph clearer. These questions may be divided into three types:

1. General paragraph organization.

2. Adding new information to the paragraph.

3. Combination of sentences.

Strategies:

1. Read the entire passage quickly for the overall idea and tone.

2. Read the question.

3. Reread the relevant portion of the paragraph (and its context which means read a line or two before and after).

4. Predict the correction.

5. Check for an error-less match.

The ACT Reading Test

The reading section will include both single and paired passages. On the ACT, there are about 10 questions per passage or set of paired passages.

Common Types of Reading Questions:

ACT reading questions fall into one of three categories: "key ideas and details" questions, "craft and structure" questions, or questions on the "integration of knowledge and ideas." Within these categories, you will see questions that ask you to do the following:

1. **Identify and interpret specific details within the passage:** These questions are often the most straightforward and require you to refer to specific things mentioned in the text.

2. **Determine a main idea**: These questions may refer to a specific sentence, paragraph, or the passage as a whole. You may need to look at "the big picture" as opposed to focusing on specific details.

3. **Understand comparisons and contrasts:** These questions will ask how ideas relate to each other in the passage and are most common in paired passages.

4. **Understand cause and effect**: These questions require students to recognize the relationship between actions within a text. Sometimes you will have to replace a "cause" or "effect" with something more logical or in-line with what the text is focusing on.

5. **Make generalizations:** These questions often require you to summarize or interpret content within the passage.

6. **Vocabulary in context:** These questions will ask about the denotations or connotations of vocabulary found in the passage. Questions will often refer to specific lines in the text. Remember, many words have more than one meaning; it is the meaning appropriate to the passage that you must identify.

7. **Understand sequencing or plot**: Here you may have to recount the order in which events happened or place a specific reference in an appropriate paragraph.

8. **Analyze purpose and method**: Questions like these will require you to recognize the author's intentions or goals in writing the text, and may also require you to recognize what the author did to achieve those goals.

9. **Evaluate arguments**: While often seemingly straightforward, these sometimes tricky questions require you to recognize and explain persuasive arguments.

10. **Compare information across texts**: These questions are exclusive to paired passages and involve comparing or contrasting the content in the paired passages.

Steps to Answer ACT Reading Questions:

Single Passages:

1. Always begin with the introductory text at the top of the reading; this little blurb will provide you with useful background information.

2. Begin to read the passage actively. Underline important points, and make notations in the margins. Read for general understanding and overall structure/plot.

3. Always make sure to read all of the text in each paragraph, even if you are not reading closely. Skimming the passage and searching for answers is not a good approach. Realize that everything is important.

4. Read the question while covering up the answers to the question.

5. Before looking at the answer choices, predict a good answer.

6. Check the answer choices to see which, if any, are similar to your prediction.

7. Use the process of elimination.

Paired Passages:

Paired passages are two reading passages that have a common theme or subject. The ACT will ask questions based on each of the passages individually and in relation to each other.

1. Read the first passage.

2. Answer questions dealing only with the first passage (probably the first three or four).

3. Read the second passage.

4. Answer questions dealing only with the second passage (usually three or four).

5. Finally, answer the questions that compare the passages (usually three or four).

Remember:

1. Do not make assumptions or judgments from your own personal experience; all answers are in the passages or may be directly inferred from the passages. In some cases, the answers may be nearly word-for-word in the text.

2. Pay attention to details! Harder questions will ask about specific details while giving extraneous or non-relevant but text-accurate options as incorrect answer choices.

Watch out for the following clues:

1. Words signaling a change/contrast/antonym:

- but	- yet	- since	- unless
- due to	- oddly	- because	- moreover
- curiously	- however	- although	- ironically
-uncharacteristically	- strangely	- in spite of	- nonetheless
- on the contrary	- on the other hand	- even so	- nevertheless
- while	- conversely	- despite	- not
- in contrast	- even though	- rather than	

2. Words showing comparison/synonyms:

- and	- too	- along with	- similarly
- alike/like	- plus	- also	- commonly
- or			

General Language Arts Tips

Grammar rules to know for the exams: Most common grammar, punctuation, and syntax questions and tips

1. Know your homophones (words that sound the same but mean different things). Here are some of the most commonly confused ones to get you started:

    a. fare/fair

    b. cite/sight/site

    c. there/they're/their

    d. it's/its

    e. then/than

    f. compliment/complement

    g. your/you're

    h. rite/write/right

    i. affect/effect

    j. peak/peek/pique

    k. brake/break

    l. bear/bare

    m. allowed/aloud

    n. allusion/illusion/elusion

2. Eliminate redundancy. Being concise is usually better. If adding words does not clarify meaning or correct a grammatical error, then do not add them—even if you think it "sounds smarter that way."

3. Keep verb tenses consistent and use parallel structure.

> **Incorrect:** My dog not only lik**es** to play fetch, but also lik**ed** to chase cars.
>
> **Incorrect:** My dog not only likes play**ing** fetch, but he also likes **to chase** cars.
>
> **Correct:** My dog not only lik**es** play**ing** fetch, but he also lik**es** chas**ing** cars.

4. If a clause or phrase can be removed without changing the meaning of the sentence, then it should be surrounded by a pair of commas (or sometimes a pair of em-dashes), one at the beginning of the clause and one at the end. If removing the phrase changes the meaning, you should NOT use commas.

> **Incorrect:** People, who dislike loud music, won't enjoy rock concerts.
>
> **Correct:** People who dislike loud music won't enjoy rock concerts.
>
> **Incorrect:** I love the Harry Potter books which are full of adventure because they offer an escape from the dullness of everyday life.
>
> **Correct:** I love the Harry Potter books, which are full of adventure, because they offer an escape from the dullness of everyday life.
>
> **Correct:** I love the Harry Potter books—which are full of adventure—because they offer an escape from the dullness of everyday life.

5. When to use a comma, semicolon, colon, or em-dash

    a. Commas (,)
        i. Separate three or more items in a list.

>   **Example:** I went to the store to buy milk, apples, bread, and carrots.

        ii. Separate independent clauses (phrases that could be complete sentences) when the second clause has a FANBOYS (For, And, Nor, But, Or, Yet, So) conjunction

Incorrect: It was raining all day, I didn't go hiking.

Correct: It was raining all day, <u>so</u> I didn't go hiking.

  iii. Set off introductory information

    Example: During the production of the film, the star actress nearly quit.

  iv. Set off nonessential descriptive information using a **pair** of commas **(see #4)**

  v. Are used to set off a transition word (*however, therefore, for example, on the other hand,* etc.) at the beginning of a sentence. A pair of commas is used to set off a transition word in the middle of a sentence.

    Example 1: However, my sister refused to help me move the furniture.

    Example 2: My sister, however, refused to help me move the furniture.

 b. Semicolons (;)

  i. Join two independent clauses (aka complete sentences) **without** a FANBOYS conjunction. The clauses on both sides of the semicolon must both be able to work as complete, stand-alone sentences. Remember: as far as correct usage is concerned, a semicolon is interchangeable with a period.

    Incorrect: It was raining all day; <u>so</u> I didn't go hiking.

    Correct: It was raining all day; I didn't go hiking.

 c. Colons (:)

  i. Introduce lists or explanations

  ii. **Must come after an independent clause** (complete sentence). If there is not an independent clause, you cannot use a colon there.

    Incorrect: My two favorite hobbies are: skiing and reading.

    Correct: I have two favorite hobbies: skiing and reading.

 d. Em-dashes (—)

  i. Indicate a significant pause or break in thought and add emphasis. They can also be used in the same way as either a colon or a semicolon.

    Example: The message of this book is simple—study hard for your SAT.

  ii. Set off explanatory examples or information from the rest of the sentence when used in a pair **(see #4)**

6. Pay attention to subject-verb agreement and pronoun-antecedent (aka the pronoun and what it is referring to) agreement

Incorrect: <u>People</u> often like parties because **<u>he</u>** gets to see **<u>his</u>** friends.

Incorrect: <u>People</u> often **<u>likes</u>** parties because they get to see their friends.

Correct: People often like parties because they get to see their friends.

7. Apostrophes

   a. Indicate possession: 's for singular nouns, s' for plural nouns

      Examples: Julia's phone, my friends' cars

   b. Create contractions

      Examples: who is = who's, there is = there's, it is = it's

8. Modifiers must be next to what they're modifying (avoid "dangling modifiers"). The subject of the sentence <u>must</u> immediately follow the modifier. Think: what or whom is being described? Does the wording of the sentence make that clear?

   Incorrect: Having arrived late for class, **<u>a written excuse</u>** was needed.

   Correct: Having arrived late for class, **<u>the student</u>** needed a written excuse.

9. Which vs. that: Which one is correct? Do I need a comma?

   a. If you are using "which," you need to use a comma because "which" is used to introduce non-essential descriptive information.

      Example: My bike, which has a flat tire, is in the garage.

      This sentence simply describes the bike and identifies its location; there's no implication that the speaker owns more than one bike.

   b. If you are using "that," you are describing and defining the noun that comes before it and introducing essential information that cannot be separated from that noun. Therefore, you should not use a comma.

      Example: My bike that has a flat tire is in the garage.

      This sentence implies that the speaker has more than one bike, and the one with a broken wheel is in the garage.

10. Run-on sentences and sentence fragments

    a. Make sure the sentence has a subject, a verb, expresses a complete thought, and makes sense on its own. This is a complete sentence, or an **independent clause**. If the sentence has two independent clauses, you can join them with a comma and a FANBOYS conjunction **(see 5.a.ii)**. Alternatively, you can split the two clauses with either a period or a semicolon **(see 5.b)**.

Incorrect: I love to write short stories. I would write one every day if I had the time. These sentences are the same as the last group of "Correct" sentences.

Correct: I love to write short stories, and I would write one every day if I had the time.

Correct: I love to write short stories; I would write one every day if I had the time.

Correct: I love to write short stories. I would write one every day if I had the time.

b. If a clause lacks a subject, verb, or does not make sense on its own, then it is incorrect and considered a sentence fragment, and is not a complete sentence. It must either be attached to an independent clause with a comma or be corrected in such a way that it becomes an independent clause.

Incorrect: Because his car was in the shop.

Correct: Because his car was in the shop, he had to take the bus to work.

Correct: He had to take the bus to work because his car was in the shop.

Chapter 4

The ACT Writing Test (Essay)

In this chapter:

- The ACT Writing Test (Essay)
- Writing Preparation for the ACT Essay – Overview
- Sample ACT Passages for Analysis
- Practice Worksheets: Analysis and Outlining
- Professional Tutoring, LLC, ACT Essay Scoring Rubric
- Sample Student Essays in response to published ACT Prompts

ACT Essay Overview

The ACT Writing Test (Essay)

In the ACT Writing Test, students are tested on their analytical writing ability. They are asked to write a persuasive essay requiring them to take a position on an issue. Students are given a short (~100 word) overview of an issue, followed by three different perspectives on that issue. They are then asked to choose their own perspective on the issue and discuss the relationship between the perspective they chose and the other two perspectives provided.

What You'll Do

- Complete the essay in 40 minutes.

- Read the 100-word overview and the three short opinions on a continuum.

- Analyze and relate the three different perspectives on a specific issue to each other and to your own opinion.

- Graded on:

- Ideas and Analysis
- Development and Support
- Organization
- Language Use and Conventions.

Scoring

The ACT essay is scored from 2-12 in each of the four categories listed above; the scores are then averaged for a final score out of 12.

Learning to work on the ACT Essay

The ACT essay requires you to have a deep understanding of how arguments are constructed. The purpose of this chapter is to teach you how to write successful ACT essays. For your convenience, we have broken down these essays for you in a step-by-step and paragraph-by-paragraph format. There were no published rubrics for the essays available, so we have created our own, which you will find at the end of the chapter.

Writing Preparation for the ACT Essay - Overview

The purpose of the ACT essay is to evaluate your ability to understand, analyze AND relate three different perspectives on a specific issue to each other and to your specific opinion. The perspectives will include a far left, middle of the road, and far right opinion on a continuum. The ACT essay asks you to take a stance on the issue outlined in the prompt (~100 words) and compare your perspective to the three different views (~ 30 words per perspective) offered with the prompt. Www.ACT.org states that the ACT Essay requires "critical engagement" and "asks students to develop an argument that puts their own perspective in dialogue with [perspectives of] others."

Graders will evaluate your writing on the four domains listed below (paraphrased from www.ACT.org).

Domain (Grading Criteria)	Students' Writing Goal
Ideas and Analysis:	Demonstrate understanding of multiple perspectives - Generate ideas and use reasoning to support various perspectives including the student's viewpoint
Development and Support:	Clear discussion of ideas, rationale, and argument
	Student guides the reader through his/her argument with examples to support points

Student will evaluate the implications/consequences of his/her argument or proposed changes

** From Professional Tutoring: You must

- Refute the author's argument(s)

- Establish and refute counterarguments

- Relate each of the three examples to your position

Organization: Ideas are organized logically with clarity and purpose

Logical ordering guides the reader through the student's discussion

Language Use and Conventions: Demonstrate writing ability through the correct usage of grammar, syntax, word usage, and mechanics

Use of an appropriate, understandable tone

Since not all students opt to complete the ACT essay, your essay score will be separate from your ACT Composite Score. You will receive a total of five scores for this test: a score in each of the four domains listed above, which are then averaged together to generate a single subject-level writing score. Each of your domain scores will range from 2-12, as will your total essay score.

To provide students with more detailed guidance, Professional Tutoring developed an ACT Essay Scoring Rubric (provided later in this chapter).

Part I: Critical Thinking and Writing Preparation

In the ACT Essay, you will demonstrate your ability to use different literary devices, evidence, and persuasive techniques to most effectively persuade your reader of your point of view.

A. Analytical and Writing Skills:

1. Critical Reasoning:

_____

_____

_____

Purpose and Examples:

_____

_____

_____

2. Refutation:

_____

_____

_____

Purpose and Examples:

_____

_____

_____

3. Academic Argument:

_____

_____

Purpose and Examples:

4. Academic Counterargument:

Purpose and Examples:

5. Spectrum of Ideas:

<u>Purpose and Examples:</u>

_____

_____

_____

6. Sequencing of Arguments:

_____

_____

_____

<u>Purpose and Examples:</u>

_____

_____

_____

B. Types of Evidence:

In the ACT essay, you will provide factual evidence to support your argument. What are different types of evidence that you could use? Is one type of evidence more credible than others? Think about where you would find this evidence.

1. What is the purpose of using evidence in an academic essay?

_____

_____

_____

2. Direct Quotes:

_____

_____

_____

Purpose in an argument essay:

_____

_____

_____

3. Academic Examples: History, Literature, Science, Current Events:

_____

_____

_____

Examples, familiar to you:

_____

_____

_____

How could you use these examples?

_____

_____

_____

C. Writing Skills

Logical Sequencing

In order for your essay to be persuasive and build your argument, you must use powerful language and logically sequence your ideas.

1. What does logical sequencing in creating a written argument mean to you? Why do you use it?

_____

_____

_____

_____

Part II: Unpacking the Prompt

General ACT Prompt:

Write a unified, coherent essay in which you evaluate multiple perspectives on the given topic. In your essay, be sure to:

1. Analyze and evaluate the perspectives given;

2. State and develop your own perspective on the issue; and

3. Explain the relationship between your perspective and those given.

Your perspective may be in full agreement with any of the others, in partial agreement, or wholly different. Whatever the case, support your ideas with logical reasoning and detailed, persuasive examples.

The ACT gives you these further instructions/hints on the pages provided for your prewriting:

Planning Your Essay

(Exact ACT Exam Instructions)

Your work on these prewriting pages will not be scored.

Use the space below and on the back cover to generate ideas and plan your essay. You may wish to consider the following as you think critically about the task:

Significance of the overview:

- Historical

- Cultural

- Literary

- Science

- Current Events

Strengths and weaknesses of the three given perspectives:

- What insights do they offer, and what do they fail to consider?

- Why might they be persuasive to others, or why might they fail to persuade?

Your own knowledge, experience, and values:

- What is your perspective on this issue, and what are its strengths and weaknesses?

- How will you support your perspective in your essay?

Preparing to write:

In your own words, explain what the ACT is asking you to do in your 40-minute essay.

_____

_____

_____

_____

Part III: Writing – Steps to Success

1. Carefully read the prompt and all three of the given perspectives. It is important that you fully understand what all three of the perspectives are arguing.

2. Evaluate the overview.

   - What is the general topic?

   - Jot down some facts about the topic in general. What is the history of this issue? Make connections: culture, economics, sociology, psychology, personal experience. This will become your introduction and carry you through the essay. You will also tie the essay together in your conclusion and return to these details.

3. Re-read the three perspectives to create your essay argument and outline.

   - Lay out the three arguments in a logical sequence from left to right from one extreme to the other, along a spectrum.

   - Jot down positive and negative points for each perspective.

   - Jot down an argument (you may paraphrase the author's argument) and counterargument for each example (you must have your own).

   - Evaluate: Does one position resonate the most with you?

   - Which position would be the easiest for you to support? This is the one which you will defend in your essay.

   - Why does your chosen perspective make more sense than the others?

   - Brainstorm evidence supporting your position. Although the ACT does not deduct points for factually inaccurate information, do not blatantly falsify your data points.

   - Brainstorm counterarguments to your position and your own refutations of these counterarguments.

4. Consider the tone you want to convey - you are trying to persuade your reader that your opinion is the right one, so it's okay to be more passionate and perhaps take a slightly less formal tone.

5. Do NOT even think about writing before taking at least five minutes to complete steps 1, 2, and 3.

6. Timing: 5 minutes: Brainstorm ideas and evidence, outline

     30 minutes: Write your essay

     5 minutes: Proofread

7. Write your thesis. You should state exactly what position you are arguing and which perspectives you agree/disagree with.

8. Create a five-paragraph outline, as per these worksheets.

9. Try to write your essay in the approximately 30 minutes you will have after the outlining. Make sure to leave time to proofread.

10. As you write, keep the following in mind:

   - Write formally – Five paragraphs, academic diction, no contractions, no second person and minimal first person.

   - Use academic vocabulary correctly; use words that you know well. Advanced vocabulary sounds very stilted (awkward) when not used correctly.

   - Use transitional sentences between paragraphs as you change from one point to the next. This will help readers follow your arguments.

   - Remember: If your evidence does not clearly and directly relate to your thesis, you should not include it in your essay.

11. Re-read what you have written. Does it effectively answer the questions? Is it logically sequenced? Does your evidence strongly and directly support your thesis and arguments? Does it have the tone you wanted to convey? Is it clearly written? Check for grammatical and spelling errors.

12. Score yourself using the Professional Tutoring ACT Essay Rubric on pages 20-21.

Sample ACT Passages for Analysis

I.   Liberal Arts

For thousands of years, educated people have studied the liberal arts as part of an academic curriculum. This curriculum has included areas of study such as history, religion, philosophy, literature, music, art, and foreign, and ancient languages. During this time, it was thought that a well-rounded person must be fluent in these subjects and that humans had much to learn from the arts and previous societies. However, in the twenty-first century, some people argue that the liberal arts are no longer necessary because our society's culture is now based upon technological and business advancements. The liberal arts are sometimes seen as suitable for those with money and time to spare, suited for a dalliance or something to study in free time, but not worthy of study as careers or even as supports to other careers.

Read and carefully consider these perspectives. Each suggests a way of thinking about the changing value of the liberal arts in our culture.

Perspective One	Perspective Two	Perspective Three
The liberal arts have lost their value in our technology-based society and should not be required in an academic curriculum. Areas of study need to be relevant and lead to an individual obtaining a job.	Some of the liberal arts are important and should be studied. We need to know history and how to effectively read and write, but otherwise, the liberal arts are too expensive to study if they do not lead to a job.	The liberal arts allow us to experience and understand our human condition and are vital to being a well-rounded person and society.

Essay Task

Write a unified, coherent essay in which you evaluate multiple perspectives on the changing value of the liberal arts in our society. In your essay, be sure to:

- Analyze and evaluate the perspectives given;

- State and develop your own perspective on the issue; and

- Explain the relationships between your perspective and those given

Your perspective may be in full agreement with any of the others, in partial agreement, or wholly different. Whatever the case, support your ideas with logical reasoning and detailed, persuasive examples.

II.   Social Media

Social media is now so ubiquitous that it is an everyday part of many Americans' lives, consuming many hours a day for some people. As social media has increased our ability to connect with others who share our lives and our interests, it has also resulted in unintended negative consequences such as cyberbullying, attention issues, and "wasted" time. Some might say that the ability to stay in touch with those far away and to share our interests with the entire world offset the negatives, but others might say that we are too connected and that social media is impacting our ability to interact with those people right in front of us. It is clear that social media has dramatically changed our lives, and we need to consider its benefits as well as its disadvantages.

Read and carefully consider these perspectives. Each suggests a way of thinking about the impact of social media on our lives.

Perspective One	Perspective Two	Perspective Three
Social media has increased our ability to interact with our family and friends as well as others who share our interests.	Social media gives everyone a voice and allows shy, introverted people to participate in social rituals and express themselves. It also allows for the creation of political movements and community organizing.	Social media has ruined personal relationships and leads to shallow relationships. It takes people away from socializing in person and instead allows them to connect with others behind a computer screen.

Essay Task

Write a unified, coherent essay in which you evaluate multiple perspectives on the impact of social media on our lives. In your essay, be sure to:

Analyze and evaluate the perspectives given

State and develop your own perspective on the issue

Explain the relationships between your perspective and those given

Your perspective may be in full agreement with any of the others, in partial agreement, or wholly different. Whatever the case, support your ideas with logical reasoning and detailed, persuasive examples.

Practice Worksheets: Analysis and Outlining

In the ACT essay, brainstorming and outlining is possibly the most important step of your writing process. You are not just being graded on your writing ability, but also on the nuance, depth, and insight of your ideas. Sound reasoning that considers **all** of the perspectives is key. The organizational structure of your essay should enhance the flow of your essay and aid the reader in following the logic of your arguments.

Recommended ACT Essay Outline:

1. Introduction: Overview of the issue; cite history, literature, science, current events, etc. Why is this background important? Transition to the modern era and address all three perspectives briefly. End with your thesis (your position).

2. Body Paragraph 1:   Transition into the argument with which you disagree most strongly. Give the text's example or another example and address why you disagree.

3. Body Paragraph 2:   Transition into the next argument with which you disagree. Address the text's example or other example and why you disagree.

4. Body Paragraph 3:   Transition into the argument with which you agree. State the text's argument, give an example, and explain why you agree. Also present a counterargument to your position and refute it to show why your position is more valid.

5. Conclusion: Return to your central argument, re-stating the overview from your introduction.

Prompt:

Introduction: In your introduction, include a clear beginning that addresses the background or context of the issue. You may include a sentence or two using points from history, literature, current events, science, etc.

_____

_____

_____

Transition into the modern era. How does the issue present itself today and how is it relevant to modern life?

_____

_____

_____

Address all three perspectives briefly and how they relate to our modern era:

_____

_____

_____

Transition into and state your thesis (your position on the issue):

_____

_____

_____

Body Paragraph 1: In this paragraph you will address the issue with which you disagree most strongly.

Transition into and state the text's argument:

_____

_____

_____

Give an example from the given perspective or from current events (you should use a paraphrase or direct quote if relevant and possible):

_____

_____

_____

Now, counter the text's argument and explain why you disagree with it:

_____

_____

_____

Body Paragraph 2: In this paragraph you will address the other argument with which you disagree.

Transition into and state the text's argument:

_____

_____

_____

Give an example from the author's perspective or from current events (you should use a paraphrase or direct quote if relevant and possible):

_____

_____

_____

Counter the text's argument and explain why you disagree with it:

_____

_____

_____

Body Paragraph 3: In this paragraph you will summarize and explain your perspective in detail.

Transition into and state the text's argument:

_____

_____

_____

Give an example from the text's perspective or from current events (you should use a paraphrase or direct quote if relevant and possible):

_____

_____

_____

Explain why you agree with this position:

_____

_____

_____

Explain the counterargument (why someone might disagree with your position):

_____

_____

Refute the counterargument (why your position is better):

_____

_____

_____

Paragraph 5: Conclusion: In the conclusion, it is important to have a sense of completeness. Make sure to avoid introducing new ideas. Instead, focus on reiterating the main points and thesis. Restate your thesis.

_____

_____

_____

_____

_____

_____

Part V- Self-Evaluation

In general, how did you do?

_____

_____

_____

Introduction: Did you give background/context and address the modern implications of this issue? Yes or No (circle). Did you briefly state all three perspectives and clearly state your position? Yes or No (circle)

First body paragraph: Did you address the perspective with which you most strongly disagree by presenting the argument, giving an example, and countering the argument? Yes or No (circle). Describe below.

Perspective:

_____

_____

_____

Example:

_____

_____

_____

Counterargument:

_____

_____

_____

Second body paragraph: Did you address the second perspective with which you disagree by presenting the argument, giving an example, and countering the argument? Yes or No (circle). Describe below.

Perspective:

_____

_____

_____

Example:

_____

_____

_____

_____

_____

Counterargument:

_____

_____

_____

Third body paragraph: Did you address the issue with which you agree by presenting the argument, giving an example, stating why you agree, countering the argument, and refuting the argument? Yes or No (circle). Describe below.

Perspective:

_____

_____

_____

Example:

_____

_____

_____

Counterargument:

_____

_____

_____

Refutation:

_____

_____

_____

Conclusion: Did you reiterate your main points and end with a summary of your thesis?

Yes or No (circle one)

Professional Tutoring, LLC, ACT Essay Scoring Rubric.

Grading Category	Yes	Comments
Ideas and Analysis (12 points total)		
Precise, clear thesis		
Takes a position on the issue		
Evaluates all three perspectives		
Compares multiple perspectives		
Analyzes implications & underlying assumptions of perspectives		
Shows nuanced understanding of all 3 given perspectives		
Shows clear understanding of issue		
Ideas are relevant to the situation and to one another		
Analyzes relationship between the 3 perspectives		
Analysis is nuanced and insightful, not obvious or overly simplistic		
Perspectives are placed in context		
IDEAS & ANALYSIS SCORE		__/12
Development and Support (12 points total)		
Uses logical reasoning		
Ideas are clearly connected		
Arguments are not vague or repetitive		
Considers opposing viewpoints and objections		
Discussion of qualifications and complications of ideas		
Every claim made is supported by evidence or reasoning		
Gives at least 2 detailed examples		
Examples are relevant to issue and strengthen argument		
Evidence given is thoroughly explained		
DEVELOPMENT & SUPPORT SCORE		__/12
Organization (12 points total)		
5 paragraphs		
Clear introductory paragraph that states thesis		
3 body paragraphs with separate topics		
Clear conclusion		
Transitional sentences between each paragraph		
The examples follow the order in the introduction		
Transitions between ideas within paragraphs		
Ideas and evidence follow a logical sequence		

Essay is clearly unified by one main idea		
Each paragraph relates back to thesis		
Organizational structure enhances comprehension of argument		
ORGANIZATION SCORE		__/12
Language Use (12 points total)		
Uses present verb tense for literature		
Uses past tense for history		
Uses consistent verb tense for argument		
Uses parallelism		
Does not use contractions		
Does not use second person		
Appropriate tone and style		
Mostly active, minimal passive voice		
Varies sentence structure		
Uses correct spelling		
Uses punctuation correctly		
Subjects and verbs agree		
Nouns/Subject and pronouns agree		
Strong grasp of words' denotation/connotation		
Mature vocabulary		
Vocabulary does not "overwhelm" the essay		
Uses advanced techniques, e.g. "Rule of Three"		
Uses figurative language to strengthen argument		
Demonstrates proofreading		
LANGUAGE USE SCORE		__/12
Essay Grade (average of 4 category scores)		__/12
Additional Comments		

Sample Student Essays in response to published ACT prompts

The following essays are examples of responses to published ACT prompts, written by Professional Tutoring students. The Professional Tutoring staff have polished them up and modified them slightly, so that they better reflect what a "perfect" essay would look like.

ACT Essay

1. *"Free Music"*

2. *"Vocational Education"*

ACT Essay – Writing Sample – Exam #1: *"Free Music"*

Music has changed both in style and accessibility throughout the years. Hundreds of years ago music was something that was only accessible to the wealthy with any frequency, but with the advancement of technology, music has become much more easily available than it used to be. Anyone can open up Spotify, Pandora, or YouTube and listen to all of the free music they want. Some think that this has lessened the value of music in some way, but I believe it has in fact led people to appreciate music more, and has helped more people discover new artists.

There are those who say that because music is so plentiful and either very cheap or free, it has lost value. This way of thinking implies that people appreciate music less because of the lower price and higher availability. I think this is incorrect. With more and more free music coming our way, people are more inclined to access it and listen to it. People listen to music in the car, when they are getting ready, at parties, at restaurants, or just alone in their homes. They are relating to more music, and will most likely continue to search for more relatable songs, often by new artists. More people listening to, discovering, and engaging with music in no way lessens its value. If anything, it increases it, because music has become such an indispensable part of so many people's lives.

Another perspective on music is that although we still value it, it is competing with other forms of entertainment for our attention. This insinuates that people would rather spend their time and money on these other types of entertainment. But these other forms of entertainment, such as movies, television, and video games, all use music in some way, even if it is only as a background. Jaws or Star Wars would seem totally different without the soundtracks. Music is not competing with other forms of entertainment; it is enhancing them. Spending money on video games or movies does not mean we value music less.

In reality, having more music available has only increased appreciation for it. More people have the opportunity to discover new artists, and fall in love with new favorite bands. They can listen to more than just the same thirty songs repeating on the radio, without spending money not in their budget. This is a good thing, and it has increased many people's appreciation for music. Although some might argue that this lower price means music has lower value, economic value is not the same as cultural value. Free sources can only help the value of music to grow.

At the end of the day, music always has had and always will have value in our society. Lower prices and other forms of affordable entertainment have not changed this. Getting our music for free has only increased its value to our culture.

ACT Essay – Writing Sample – Exam #2: *"Vocational Education"*

Vocational skills are skills that are needed when learning a trade and getting a job. Schools require certain academic courses, but there is a debate on whether vocational skill classes should also be provided at schools. Although some do believe that career-training classes are helpful to those who do not excel academically, vocational skill classes should not be offered at public schools.

The belief that career classes will help some students who are not successful in academic classes is valid, however, academic classes will help in all fields of jobs and are good, and often necessary, to have as background knowledge. In contrast, career classes focus on only one thing or skill, which does not help students broaden their horizons to find new interests, and will not serve them well if they ever change their choice of career. Additionally, students should be pushed to do better in their academic classes instead of being encouraged to replace them with specific vocational training. Even if they do end up in the exact careers they trained for, they will probably need the skills their academic classes were trying to teach them.

Another point of view is that skilled workers require knowledge and advanced communication skills, which are learned in academic classes. This belief is accurate and reasonable. Every job requires these types of skills, and academic courses are what teach these skills to students most effectively, thus preparing them for all possible careers. For example, English classes teach students how to read critically and how to write; two skills that are needed for almost every job out there. Most jobs require a person to use at least some basic math skills, and understanding current events requires a basic understanding of history and government. Vocational classes are not designed to teach students these fundamental skills, and are too narrowly focused to do this properly. The skills learned in vocational classes cannot replace the knowledge that needs to be acquired through academics.

One last argument for schools to focus on academics instead of vocational training is that no one knows what jobs will look like or require in the future. For example, there may not be a need for someone to carve wood to make a bench if a machine can be used to achieve the same level of quality. In addition, many jobs will come about that do not exist right now. Training a student in a particular area will not be beneficial because the job may not be necessary in the future, which wastes both the student's time as well as the school's budget. Career-based courses are more expensive than academic courses because they are more hands-on and require more resources and equipment. That money could be better spent providing more resources for core academic classes.

In conclusion, career classes that provide vocational skills are not beneficial to a school or its students and will only be a waste of time and money. Although the classes give a student further insight into a job, they will not help if the student does not choose that job as their career or if that job is not needed in the future. As technology advances, fewer jobs are needed to do certain tasks; therefore, a student should not look into the specifics of a technical profession until college. Academic courses offer a broad enough curriculum to allow students to explore different interests, and give them enough background knowledge to prepare them for whatever their future will look like.

Vocabulary Review

SAT and ACT Vocabulary Exercise Instructions

Vocabulary study and improvement is vital for the Critical Reading and Writing sections of the SAT Exam. It is also the most boring and tedious part of SAT/ACT Preparation. I always think of studying vocabulary like doing sit ups. Sit-ups are boring and somewhat painful, but they do pay off in core strengthening. Vocabulary review will strengthen your core SAT/ACT knowledge.

The SAT has been re-designed to be more like the ACT, and now focuses on "high-utility academic words and phrases", or "Tier Two" vocabulary. These Tier Two words appear in many different texts across different domains, and they often have multiple meanings, which makes understanding the context in which they are used even more important. Included in this text are 15 vocabulary lists that include the *365 Most Frequent SAT Vocabulary Words.*

For each Vocabulary Unit, complete the "definitions" page by writing the definition in the space provided. Make sure to take note of words that have multiple or alternate meanings. Use your choice of traditional or online dictionary.

Vocabulary Units 1-21

Unit 1 Vocabulary

1. aberration _____

2. aloof _____

3. astray _____

4. brevity _____

5. compliment _____

6. corroborate _____

7. desolate _____

8. distinguish _____

9. engage _____

10. explicit _____

11. futile _____

12. hybrid _____

13. incline _____

14. interpretation _____

15. lethargic _____

16. meekness _____

17. noble _____

18. parenthetical _____

19. poles _____

20. proficient _____

21. rash _____

22. reserve _____

23. sequester _____

24. subservient _____

25. testament _____

Unit 2 Vocabulary

1. abolish

_____

2. altercation

_____

3. atrophy

_____

4. broach

_____

5. compose

_____

6. credence

_____

7. despoil

_____

8. diverge

_____

9. engender

_____

10. exploit

_____

11. galvanize

_____

12. hyperbole

_____

13. incontestable

_____

14. interval

_____

15. liable

_____

16. melancholy

_____

17. nostalgia

_____

18. passively

_____

19. portrayal

_____

20. profound

_____

21. rational

_____

22. residual

_____

23. shards

_____

24. substantiate

_____

25. transient

_____

Unit 3 Vocabulary

1. abridge

2. amass

3. attribute

4. burgeon

5. concede

6. crude

7. detach

8. dreary

9. engross

10. exponent

11. gauge

12. idolize

13. incredulous

14. intricate

15. lineage

16. menacing

17. notion

18. pathogen

19. postulate

20. project

21. realm

22. resignation

23. simulations

24. subversion

25. treacherous

Unit 4 Vocabulary

1. abstract _____

2. ambiguous _____

3. augment _____

4. cache _____

5. conceivable _____

6. culminate _____

7. detriment _____

8. drench _____

9. engulf _____

10. exquisite _____

11. generalize _____

12. ignominy _____

13. increments _____

14. inverse _____

15. listless _____

16. mercurial _____

17. novel _____

18. patrons _____

19. potent _____

20. prolong _____

21. reap _____

22. resolute _____

23. sinister _____

24. succinct _____

25. undermines _____

Unit 5 Vocabulary

1. accolade

2. ambivalence

3. austere

4. candid

5. condescend

6. cultivate

7. deviate

8. dubious

9. enigmatic

10. facets

11. genre

12. illusion

13. indifference

14. invocation

15. long (?)

16. meticulous

17. objective

18. penchant

19. practicality

20. prominent

21. recalcitrant

22. respite

23. skeptical

24. suffrage

25. underpins

Unit 6 Vocabulary

1. accommodate

2. anecdote

3. authenticate

4. capitulate

5. conductivity

6. cumbersome

7. devise

8. earnest

9. entail

10. facilitate

11. germane

12. imminent

13. indigenous

14. invoke

15. lucid

16. metropolis

17. obliterate

18. pensive

19. pragmatic

20. prone

21. recant

22. retrospect

23. solemn

24. sullen

25. underscore

Unit 7 Vocabulary

1. acquiesce

_____

2. anomalous

_____

3. autocrat

_____

4. capricious

_____

5. confer

_____

6. curator

_____

7. devoid

_____

8. eccentric

_____

9. entity

_____

10. fastidious

_____

11. glut

_____

12. immure

_____

13. indignation

_____

14. irksome

_____

15. lucrative

_____

16. mishap

_____

17. obscure

_____

18. perceives

_____

19. precede

_____

20. proprietor

_____

21. reciprocal

_____

22. revamp

_____

23. solicitude

_____

24. summon

_____

25. undetectable

_____

Unit 8 Vocabulary

1. acquisition
_____

2. antagonistic
_____

3. baffle
_____

4. catalyst
_____

5. congenial
_____

6. cursory
_____

7. devour
_____

8. eclipse
_____

9. enumerate
_____

10. feasible
_____

11. grandeur
_____

12. impartial
_____

13. indulge
_____

14. irrefutable
_____

15. lurching
_____

16. mitigate
_____

17. obsolete
_____

18. peril
_____

19. precipitation
_____

20. prospective
_____

21. refute
_____

22. reverberate
_____

23. somber
_____

24. superficially
_____

25. undulating
_____

Unit 9 Vocabulary

1. adhere

2. antipathy

3. bare

4. cease

5. conjure

6. cynic

7. diffuse

8. edict

9. ephemeral

10. feign

11. grandiose

12. imperative

13. industrious

14. jargon

15. magnanimous

16. mode

17. obstinacy

18. perpetual

19. precipitous

20. prosperous

21. relentless

22. reverence

23. sovereign

24. surge

25. unfounded

Unit 10 Vocabulary

1. admonish

2. apathy

3. barren

4. celestial

5. consecrate

6. daunt

7. digress

8. eloquent

9. epitome

10. ferocity

11. gratify

12. imperceptible

13. inevitable

14. judicious

15. malicious

16. modest

17. obstruct

18. persecuted

19. precise

20. protagonists

21. relevant

22. revive

23. sparse

24. surreptitious

25. unprecedented

Unit 11 Vocabulary

1. adversarial

2. appall

3. befall

4. censure

5. consensus

6. debilitate

7. diligence

8. embellish

9. erratic

10. fidelity

11. hail

12. impertinent

13. inexorable

14. jurisdiction

15. malignant

16. molding

17. odyssey

18. pervasive

19. predecessors

20. provocative

21. relish

22. rhetoric

23. spawning

24. susceptible

25. unseemly

Unit 12 Vocabulary

1. adverse

2. apprehension

3. belittle

4. chagrin

5. constitute

6. defer

7. diminish

8. embody

9. esthetic

10. fiscal

11. hardship

12. impervious

13. infer

14. juxtapose

15. malleable

16. momentous

17. omniscient

18. phenomenon

19. predominant

20. proximity

21. render

22. rudimentary

23. speculate

24. sustainable

25. urbane

Unit 13 Vocabulary

1. advocate _____

2. arcane _____

3. belligerent _____

4. cloister _____

5. construe _____

6. degrade _____

7. discord _____

8. eminent _____

9. ethereal _____

10. flank _____

11. hasten _____

12. implicit _____

13. infrastructure _____

14. kin _____

15. marginal _____

16. monotony _____

17. onerous _____

18. pinnacle _____

19. preoccupation _____

20. proxy _____

21. replenish _____

22. satiate _____

23. squalid _____

24. symbolic _____

25. usurp _____

Unit 14 Vocabulary

1. affiliate _____

2. aristocratic _____

3. benefactor _____

4. coalesce _____

5. consummate _____

6. delusion _____

7. discrepant _____

8. empirical _____

9. evoke _____

10. fleet _____

11. hiatus _____

12. imply _____

13. ingenious _____

14. laborious _____

15. maternal _____

16. morbid _____

17. onset _____

18. pioneering _____

19. preposterous _____

20. prudent _____

21. replete _____

22. satire _____

23. stark _____

24. synthetic _____

25. utmost _____

Unit 15 Vocabulary

1. affirm

2. arouse

3. benevolent

4. coherent

5. contingent

6. demean

7. disdain

8. emulate

9. evolve

10. flourish

11. hinder

12. impose

13. inherent

14. labyrinthine

15. mature

16. mundane

17. oppression

18. pious

19. prescribed

20. pungent

21. replicate

22. scorn

23. static

24. tact

25. vantage

Unit 16 Vocabulary

1. aggregate

2. array

3. benign

4. colloquial

5. continuum

6. demographic

7. dismay

8. enclave

9. exacerbate

10. foreseeable

11. homage

12. impudent

13. inquire

14. laden

15. maxim

16. municipal

17. ornate

18. pity

19. presided

20. qualitative

21. repose

22. scrutinize

23. stellar

24. tangent

25. veer

Unit 17 Vocabulary

1. agitate

2. articulate

3. bequeath

4. combative

5. convene

6. depict

7. disparage

8. encroach

9. exclusion

10. franchise

11. hone

12. inadvertent

13. insatiable

14. lament

15. means

16. naïve

17. ostentatious

18. plausible

19. presumption

20. quasi

21. repressed

22. secluded

23. stratosphere

24. tangible

25. venerable

Unit 18 Vocabulary

1. allegory

2. ascertain

3. besiege

4. commodity

5. conventional

6. deplete

7. disparate

8. endow

9. exemplify

10. frank

11. humane

12. inalienable

13. insolent

14. latent

15. measured

16. nefarious

17. overt

18. plight

19. prevailing

20. querulous

21. repudiates

22. seek

23. subjugate

24. tedious

25. venture

Unit 19 Vocabulary

1. alleviate

2. assert

3. bias

4. compensate

5. converge

6. deposit

7. dispense

8. endure

9. exert

10. fraudulent

11. humble

12. incendiary

13. intact

14. latitudes

15. mediation

16. negligible

17. panacea

18. plumes

19. principle

20. quirk

21. rescind

22. sensory

23. subordinate

24. tenuous

25. veritable

Unit 20 Vocabulary

1. allude

2. assess

3. blatant

4. compile

5. correlate

6. derision

7. disposition

8. enfranchise

9. expedite

10. fuse

11. hurtle

12. incite

13. integrate

14. laud

15. medium

16. nexus

17. paradox

18. poignant

19. pristine

20. ramified

21. reservations

22. sentinels

23. subsequently

24. terrestrial

25. viable

Unit 21 Vocabulary

1. virtually

2. volition

3. waned

4. wary

5. wily

6. won't

7. yearning

8. yield

Chapter 6

Introduction to the SAT and ACT Math Sections

In this chapter:
• Learn to recognize types of math problems included on the SAT and ACT Exams.
• Understand what these exams expect from test-takers.
• Make sure to bring an acceptable calculator to the exam setting.
• Review helpful study tips.

Introduction to the SAT and ACT Math Sections

Both the SAT and ACT Exams evaluate students' math fluency, essentially their knowledge of Algebra I and II, Geometry and basic Trigonometry. The questions on both exams increase in a "ladder of difficulty" as students work from problem number one forward. Expect to answer simple arithmetic and algebraic questions, puzzle through complex modeling and interpretive questions and reason your way through tricky questions, particularly on the SAT Exam.

While the SAT and ACT test for very similar math topics, the tests do have several fundamental differences:

- The SAT Exam has fewer questions, approximately 44 questions in 70 minutes.

- The ACT has more questions, approximately 60 questions in 60 minutes.

- The SAT Exam is notably more reasoning-based meaning that you will have to read each question very carefully to determine what the test is asking.

- Generally, the ACT questions are simpler than those on the SAT Exam.

- The digital SAT Exam will be provided digitally with an online calculator.

- The digital SAT Exam will be adaptive meaning that after the first math module, the system will determine if the student will progress to the lower level or higher level of math questions.

- The ACT Exam remains a paper and pencil test.

- The digital SAT Exam has two different types of questions: multiple choice and free-response (grid-in).

- The ACT Exam has only multiple choice questions.

- The ACT is not yet digital and will allow students to use a calculator. The following calculators are prohibited:

    - Texas Instruments:

        - All model numbers that begin with TI-89 or TI-92

        - TI-NSpire CAS (Note: the TI-Nspire (non-CAS) is permitted)

    - Hewlett-Packard:

        - HP Prime

        - HP 48GII

        - All model numbers that begin with HP 40G, HP 49G or HP 50G

    - Casio:

        - fx-CP400 (ClassPad 400)

        - ClassPad 300 or ClassPad 330

        - Algebra fx 2.0

        - All model numbers that begin with CFX-9970C

The math concepts on both exams are similar. You can compare them in the coming pages.

The SAT Exam - Math Section has four main topic areas:

- Heart of Algebra

- Problem-Solving and Data Analysis

- Passport to Advanced Math

- Additional Topics

The Heart of Algebra will include questions on the following concepts:

- Translate word problem into a math problem

- Linear systems

- Linear equations

- Graphing including line of best fit or curve of best fit

- Numbers and Integers: whole numbers, fractions

Problem-Solving and Data Analysis will include questions on the following concepts:

- Ratios, rates and percentages, unit conversions

- Linear and exponential growth

- Basic statistics: mean, median, mode, range

- Calculating probability based on data

- Making statistical inferences

Passport to Advanced Math will include questions on the following concepts:

- Exponents and radicals

- Isolating variables and writing literal equations

- Solving quadratic equations through factoring, completing the square, quadratic formula

- Manipulating polynomials including adding, subtracting, multiplying and dividing including long division

- Solving linear systems through substitution, graphing and linear combinations

- Function notation and manipulation

- Transforming functions, graphs, etc.

- Complex (imaginary) numbers

Additional Topics will include questions on the following concepts:

- Generally Geometry

- Area, volume, perimeter

- Circumference

- Properties of parallel lines cut by a transversal

- Right triangles, pythagorean theorem, pythagorean triples, 30-60-90 triangles and ratios and 45-45-90 triangles

- Relationships between similar polygons

- Properties of circles - arc lengths, sector length, sector area

- Degree and radian measures

- Equations of circles

The ACT Exam's math section includes two major sections,

- Preparing for Higher Math

- Integrating Essential Skills.

Preparing for Higher Math comprises approximately 60% of the ACT Math Exam and will include questions on the following concepts:

- Number and Quantity

  - Demonstrate an understanding of real and imaginary number system

- Algebra

  - Solve, graph, and model multiple types of expressions

  - Equations: linear, quadratic and polynomial

  - Radicals, exponents and their related equations

  - Systems of equations including solutions

  - Simple matrices

- Functions

  - Function definition, notation, representation, and application

  - Functions will combine concepts from linear equations, radicals, piecewise functions,

  - polynomials and logarithmic functions

  - Compositions of functions

  - Translations of functions in graphing

- Statistics & Probability

  - Understand standard distributions

  - Understand and analyze data and collection methods

  - Calculate probabilities

- Geometry

  - Knowledge of shapes and solids

  - Congruence and similarity

- Surface area, volume, perimeter, circumference, sectors

- Solve for missing values in figures

- Basic trigonometry including special right triangles and curves

Integrating Essential Skills comprises about 40% of the ACT Math Section

In these types of questions, the ACT is testing your ability to interpret math questions and apply your knowledge to solve the problems. Problems may include:

- Rates and percentages

- Proportions

- Basic statistic

- Modeling to produce, interpret and understand models and their mathematical significance.

Both the SAT and ACT Exams are knowledge-based exams. Your best bet to achieving your best score is to STUDY! Below are some tips.

1. Begin with diagnostic SAT and ACT Exams - timed and scored and taken in one "real" sitting.

2. Memorize basic concepts such as slope and forms of lines, properties of triangles and parallel lines cut by a transversal.

3. Memorize basic geometry concepts:

   - Pythagorean Theorem

   - Special Right Triangles

   - Types of Triangles and Congruence theorems

   - Circle formulas: Circumference, area, sector proportions

   - Circle ratios: arcs, central angles, sectors

   - Inscribed angles

4. Practice, practice and practice some more - 2-4 hours per week for your entire junior year of high school.

5. Practice will lead to you recognizing patterns and types of questions so that you can solve them much more quickly and efficiently.

6. Learn to manage your time.

7. Practice - more practice will lead to better speed and time management.

Once you have reinforced your math knowledge and skills, you can implement strategies to approach the exam. Keep in mind, though, that no amount of strategies will save you from not having a strong understanding and knowledge of high school math. Consider the following strategies.

1. Familiarize yourself with the types of questions and patterns.

2. Always look for tricks or simple ways to solve the problem.

3. If you do not know what to do, try something!

4. Always start with factoring whenever possible.

5. Always write out your work.

6. Always draw a picture or graph, if appropriate.

7. Plug in simple numbers but never identities to start (0, -1, 1). We recommend small numbers such as 3, 4, 5, 10.

8. Work backwards from the answer if you do not see a way forward.

9. If there are fractions with an equal sign, multiply all fractions by the least common denominator to clear the fractions.

10. Use rules to guide you through the math on both tests. Note that the SAT Exam provides some basic geometry rules at the beginning of the test.

11. Realize that figures are not necessarily drawn to scale.

12. Answer EVERY question as there is no penalty on either exam for wrong answers.

13. Know your triangles and look for triangles in other figures.

Take time and care in working through the two math chapters (Chapter 7: The Heart of Algebra and Related Math Concepts and Chapter 8: Geometry).

Chapter 7

<u>Algebra and Trigonometry</u>

In this chapter:
• Introduction to the Heart of Algebra and Trigonometric Concepts.   • 19 units ranging from Basic Skills and Testing Tricks to Trigonometry.

Problem Sets

1. Basic Skills and Testing Tricks

2. Applied Arithmetic

3. Polynomials

4. Exponents

5. Radicals

    Mastery Unit A

6. Factoring

7. Fractions

8. Lines and Linear Equations

9. Graphing Linear, Quadratic, Cubic and Absolute Value Equations

10. Systems of Linear Equations

    Mastery Unit B

11. Proportions, Ratios, Percentages

12. Functions

13. Exponential Growth and Decay:

14. Imaginary Numbers

15. Basic Statistics

Mastery Unit C

16. Advanced Statistics

17. Basic Trigonometry

18. Advanced Trigonometry

Unit 1: Basic Skills and Testing Tricks

Define

Sum: _____

Difference: _____

Product: _____

Quotient: _____

Factors: _____

Digit: _____

Integers: _____

Whole Numbers: _____

Prime Numbers: _____

Rational Numbers: _____

Real Numbers: _____

Sequence: _____

Arithmetic Sequence: _____

Geometric Sequence: _____

Solve

1. $963 + 368 + 741 + 147 + 148 =$

2. $987 + 654 + 321 + 456 + 789 =$

3. 9874 + 6541 + 3210 + 1235 + 4567 =

4. 5877 + 9565+ 3232 + 4512 + 4893 =

5. 1808 - 888 =

6. 575 * 936 =

7. 7117 * 797 =

8. 4334 and 427 are factors of what product?

9. Find the product of 725 and 305.

10. What is 528 multiplied by 962?

11. $98765/39 =$

12. Find the quotient of 1024 and 16..

13. Divide 0 by 7432.

14. Divide 7432 by 0.

Order of Operations

PEMDAS stands for:

_____

_____

_____

Solve:

15. 5 (27 + 6) + 5 (-7 - 4) =

16. 4 * 6 - 11 + 6/3 =

17. 46 - (21 - 7 - 3) =

18. 9 (8 - 5)^3 =

19. 5 (5 - 0) (5 - 5) (4 - 3) =

20. $14 + 5 * 3 - 3^2$

Unit 2: Applied Arithmetic

Define

1. If a number is located at -1.5 on a number line, where is its square?

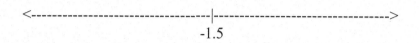
-1.5

2. Under which of the following circumstances will the sum of integers m and n always be an odd integer?

   a) m is an odd integer
   b) n is an odd integer
   c) m and n are both odd integers
   d) m and n are both even integers
   e) m is an odd integer and n is an even integer

3. What is $3.006 * 10^7$

4. What is $3.006 * 10^{-7}$

5. If 26 - x = 18, what is 4x?

6. When x = 3, what is (15+4 (6 +5x))

7. Solve for r: P=rt

8. When x = ½, what is $\dfrac{10\text{-}6x}{x}$

9. If $\dfrac{3x}{5}$ = 12, what is 4x-3?

10. Eight (8) years ago my age was $\frac{1}{4}$ of what it will be in 16 years. How old am I?

11. If $x^2 = 25$ and $x > 0$, what is the sum of $x + 6 - (3x - 7)$

12. If $(2 + 5) + (3+x) = 7$, then $x =$

13. If $5x - 2 = 13$ and $x + y = 7$, what does $y =$?

14. If $x^2 - y^2 = 8$, then $2(x^2 - y^2) =$

15. If $20x - 20y = 40$, what is: $4x - 4y =$

16. If $3x = 6$, what does $(3x + 2)^2 - 7 =$

17. If $10x + 6 = 6$, what is $5x + 3$?

18. Solve for x: $-3 (5x - 4) = 2 (5x - 1)$

19. Solve for x: $3/2 (8x - 4) - 6 = 8x - 4$

20. Black tea worth $1.50 per pound is mixed with green tea worth $1.75 per pound to obtain 10 pounds of the mixture worth $1.60 per pound. How much green tea is in the final mixture?

Algebra Unit 3: Polynomials

Define

Variable: _____

Monomial: _____

Binomial: _____

Trinomial: _____

Numerical: _____

Coefficient: _____

Base: _____

Exponent: _____

Notes

1. Make sure that variables match so that you can add or subtract the polynomials.

    e.g.: $x^3 + 2x^2 \neq 3x^5$

2. Be sure to distribute negative signs.

    e.g.: $(2x^2 - 2x - 5) - (x^2 + 8x - 12) =$
    $2x^2 - 2x - 5 - x^2 - 8x + 12 = x^2 - 10x + 7$

3. Standard form of a polynomial means that the degree of its monomial terms decreases from left to right.

Simplify and write in standard form

1. $3y + 12 + y^2 + 3y + 12$

2. $6x^2 + 5 + 3 - 2x^2$

3. $2x^2 - x + 3 + 3x^2 - 4x + 7$

4. $3(x^2 + 2xy + y^2) - 2(x^2 - y^2) + x^2 - 2xy + y^2$

5. $10x - 2(3x - (x - 2) + 3(x + 3))$

6. $y^2 + 3y^4 - (y^5 - y^4)$

7. $(x + 1)(x + 5)$

8. $(x - 3)(3x + 1)$

9. $(x + \frac{1}{4})(x - \frac{1}{2})$

10. $(x^2 + 9)(x^2 - x - 4)$

11. $(3x^2 + x - 5)(2x^2 - 5x + 4)$

12. $(x^2 + 4x - 9)(x^2 - \frac{1}{2})$

13. $-2x^2 (3x^3 - 2x^2 - 4x + 3)$

14. $(x^3y^4z^5) (3x^8yz^3)$

15. $81x^6y^5 / 27x^3y$

16. Divide $4x^2y^3$ into $(-12x^5y^8 + 8x^3y^6)$

17. $(18x^2y^3 - 48x^4y^2 + 27x^3y^4) / -3xy^2$

18. $.3 (6) / .6$

19. $(15p^2q^2 - 5pq^3 + 10p) / 5pq$

20. Simplify $-4x^3 - 12x^3 + 9x^2$

Unit 4: Exponents

Notes

1. 1. <u>Basic Rules</u>:

   $a^0 = 1$ any number $^0 = 1$

   $a^1 = a$ any number $^1 =$ itself

   $a^2 = a * a$ $a^3 = a * a * a$ (and so on)

2. <u>Addition/Subtraction</u>:   Both bases and exponents must match!

3. <u>Multiplication</u>:   Same bases, add the exponents

   $a^2 * a^5 = a^{2+5} = a^7$

   Different bases, list alphabetically by variable

   $a^2 * b^5 = a^2 b^5$

4. <u>Division</u>:   As shown in last unit, subtract exponents when bases match.

   $81x^6y^5 / 27x^3y = 3x^3y^4$

5. <u>Raising to a power</u>:   Multiply exponents

   $(a^2)^3 = a^{2 \times 3} = a^6$

6. <u>Negative Exponents</u>:   Negative exponents cause their corresponding base (number or variable) to change location from the numerator to the denominator or from the denominator to the numerator.

   $$\frac{1}{a^{-5}} = \frac{a^5}{1} \quad \text{and} \quad \frac{a^5}{1} = \frac{1}{a^5}$$

7. <u>Quotient of Powers</u>: $\left(\frac{a}{b}\right)^n = \frac{a^n}{b^n}$

8. <u>Negative Signs</u>:   Be careful of negative signs:

   $(-a)^2 = a^2$ the negative sign is in ( )

   $-a^2 = -a^2$ the negative sign is NOT in ( )

   $-(a)^2 = -a^2$ the negative sign is NOT in ( )

9. <u>Order of Operations</u>:   Always follow PEMDAS!

Positive Exponents

Solve

1. $(-9)^2$

2. $2x^2 = 32$

3. $(5^5)^4$

4. $(\frac{1}{2}x^6)^2$

5. $(3 * 7)^4$

6. $(9a^3)^2 * (2a)^3$

7. $(-3xy^2)^3 * (-2x^2y)^2$

8. $2^x = 4$

9. $2^4 = 4^x$

10. $128^{1/2} = 16^x$ What is 2^{2x}?

Negative Exponents

Rewrite the expressions with only positive exponents

11. x^{-9}

12. $5x^{-4}$

13. $(15x)^{-2}$

14. $\left(\frac{1}{4}x\right)^{-5}$

15. $3a^{-3}b^{-8}$

16. $1/(7a^{-4}b^{-1})$

Simplify

17. $(81a^{-6}b^5) / (27a^9b^7)$

18. $(18a^2b^3 - 48a^{-4}b^{-2} + 27a^3b^4) / (-3ab^{-2})$

19. $\dfrac{6x}{18y^{-2}} \times \dfrac{y^3x}{x^3}$

20. $\dfrac{y^{10}}{2x^3} \times \dfrac{20x^{14}}{xy^3}$

Solve

21. $4^x * 4^2 = 4^5$

22. $\dfrac{x^2}{x^a} = x^5$

23. $a^{-1} = \dfrac{1}{6}$

24. $\dfrac{b^6}{6b^{-4}} \times \dfrac{12}{10b^7} = 36$

25. $(27/64)^{-2/3}$

26. $\dfrac{5.1 \times 10^{-6}}{1.7 \times 10^{-12}}$

27. Solve for x: $2^{2x+7} = 2^{17}$

28. Rewrite the expression $49x^2y^2z^2$ using only one exponent.

29. The radius of a cylinder is 7.8×10^{-4}m. The height of the cylinder is 3.4×10^{-2}m. What is the volume of the cylinder? Write your answer in scientific notation. (*hint:* $V = \pi r^2 h$)

30. A snail travels at a speed of 3.0×10^{-2} mi/h. What is the snail's speed in inches per minute?

Unit 5: Radicals

Perfect Squares

a) $1^2 =$

b) $2^2 =$

c) $3^2 =$

d) $4^2 =$

e) $5^2 =$

f) $6^2 =$

g) $7^2 =$

h) $8^2 =$

i) $9^2 =$

j) $10^2 =$

k) $11^2 =$

l) 12^2

m) $13^2 =$

n) $14^2 =$

o) 15^2

p) $16^2 =$

q) $17^2 =$

r) 18^2

s) $19^2=$

t) $20^2 =$

u) 21^2

v) $22^2 =$

w) $23^2 =$

x) 24^2

y) $25^2 =$

Notes:

1. Radicals are similar to variables. Only matching radicals may be added together. Non-matching and matching variables may be multiplied.

2. Radicals may be written with the radical ($\sqrt{}$) sign or with exponents. e.g. : $x^{1/2} = \sqrt{x}$. $x^{2/3}$

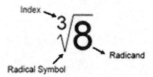

3. The index of a radical expression must always be a positive integer greater than 1. When no index is written it is assumed to be 2, or a square root.

4. Even indices yield both a positive and negative root. Odd indices yield only one root which matches the sign of the radicand.

5. Make factor trees. Circle all prime numbers.

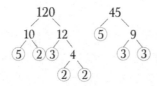

6. When a radicand in a denominator is not a perfect square, you may need to rationalize the denominator to remove the radical. Multiply the numerator by the same radical expression. Choose an expression that makes the radicand in the denominator a perfect square.

7. Be aware of the quadratic formula which will be used in Unit 5: $\dfrac{-b \pm \sqrt{b^2 - 4ac}}{2a}$

Practice Problems

Simplify

1. $\sqrt{40}$

2. $\sqrt{75}$

3. $(162)^{1/3}$

4. $125^{1/3}$

5. $16^{-3/2}$

6. $\sqrt[3]{27xy^3}$

7. $\left(6^{2/3} \times 6^{1/4}\right)^{12/11}$

8. $\sqrt{112}$ / $\sqrt{175}$

9. $\left(\frac{2}{3} * \sqrt{3}\,\right)^2$

10. $\left(2\sqrt{5}\,\right)/\sqrt{4}$

11. $\sqrt{x} = 15$

12. $\sqrt{(x + 25)} = 25$

13. $\sqrt[4]{(b + 12)} = 6$

14. $\sqrt{3x + 1} = \sqrt{x + 9}$

15. $\sqrt{3x + 6} + \sqrt{6x + 4} = 0$

16. $\sqrt{b + 12} = b + 6$

17. You throw a ball upward. Its height h, in feet, after t seconds can be modeled by the function $h = -16t^2 + 30t + 6$. After how many seconds will it hit the ground?

18. The distance, d, in miles that a person can see to the horizon can be modeled by the formula d $= \sqrt{\dfrac{3h}{2}}$ where h is the person's height above sea level in feet. To the nearest tenth of a mile, how far to the horizon can a person see if they are 100 feet above sea level? Round your answer to the nearest tenth of a mile.

19. Find the area of a rectangle with a length of $5+2\sqrt{5}$ and a width of $3+7\sqrt{5}$

20. The voltage of an iPhone speaker is V=4 $\sqrt{P}$ P is the power of the speaker. What is the voltage of a 400 watt speaker?

Mastery Unit A

1. What is $3.006 * 10^7$

2. When x = 3, what is (15+4 (6 +5x))

3. Solve for r: P=rt

4. When x = ½, what is $\dfrac{10-6x}{x}$

5. If $\dfrac{3x}{5}$ = 12, what is 4x-3?

6. What is the sum of the solutions of the 2 equations below?
   i.   5x = 25
   ii. 2y + 17 = 18

7. Solve the equation: $6x+5 = 36$

8. If $\frac{1}{y} = \sqrt{36}$, then $y =$

9. $4\sqrt{96} - 3\sqrt{216} =$

10. $(.4x^3)^2 =$

11. $\sqrt{\frac{x^2}{4} + \frac{4x^2}{9}} =$

12. $x + y = 7$ and $x^2 - y^2 = 56$, then $x - y =$

13. $x^2 - y^2 = 121$ and $x + y = 11$, then $x - y =$

14. If $20x - 20y = 40$, what is: $4x - 4y =$

15. $2\sqrt{2} \times 3\sqrt{2} =$

16. If $3x = 6$, what does $(3x + 2)^2 - 7 =$

17. If $2x + 3y = 17$ and $x + 2y = 7$, then $(3x + 5y)/2 =$

18. $7x - 4y = 24$ and $x + 12y = 40$, then $(x + y) =$

19.   If $x^2 - y^2 = 8$, then $2(x^2 - y^2) =$

20.   If $x = \dfrac{y}{5}$ and $10x = 14$, then $y =$

21. $\dfrac{7}{8} * \dfrac{8}{9} * \dfrac{9}{10} * \dfrac{10}{11} * \dfrac{11}{12} * \dfrac{12}{13} * \dfrac{13}{14} * \dfrac{14}{15} * \dfrac{15}{16} * \dfrac{16}{17} * \dfrac{17}{18}$

22.   If $x^2 = 25$ and $x > 0$, what is the sum of $x + 6 - (3x - 7)$

23.   If $\sqrt{81} + x = 324,$ *what is the value of x?*

24. $c^{5/4} = 81$, what is $5c$?

25. Simplify the following expression: $(x^2 - 64) - (x^3 + 4x^2 - 14)$

26. Factor $x^3 - 8$

27. Factor $8x^3 - 64$

28. If $x + 7 = 6$ and $x - y = 8$, what is the value of $(x - y)(x^2 - y^2)$

29. If a number is located at -2.5 on a number line, where is its square?

<--->

30. Under which of the following circumstances will the sum of integers m and n always be an odd integer?

    a) m is an odd integer
    b) n is an odd integer
    c) m and n are both odd integers
    d) m and n are both even integers
    e) m is an odd integer and and n is an even integer

Algebra Unit 6: Factoring

Notes:

1. Factoring is the opposite of foiling.

2. Make sure to take out the greatest common factor first.

3. Factoring patterns are always the same!

Difference of two squares:	$x^2 - y^2 = (x - y)(x + y)$
Sum of two squares:	Not possible w/o imaginary numbers
Sum of two cubes:	$(x^3 + y^3) = (x + y)(x^2 - xy + y^2)$
Difference of two cubes:	$(x^3 - y^3) = (x - y)(x^2 + xy + y^2)$

4. Grouping:

   Pull out the common factors, first, and then group the parentheses.
   1. Make sure that exponents are in descending order. Re-write, if necessary.
   2. Put parentheses around the 1st and 2nd terms and the 3rd and 4th terms.
   3. Pull out the common factors(s).
   4. Write the factors (in parentheses) that occur twice.
   5. Write the other two factors and the sign between them.
   e.g.: $x^3 + 2x^2 + 3x + 6 = x^2(x + 2) + 3(x + 2) = (x^2 + 3)(x + 2)$

5. Real Number Solutions of Quadratics are based on the equation's discriminant: $b^2 - 4ac$

   Discriminant $= 0$: One real solution
   Discriminant > 0: Two real solutions
   Discriminant < 0: No real solutions

Greatest Common Factor (GCF) (Simplify)

1. $7x^3$, $28x$, $14x^4$

2. $16a^2b$, $84ab^2$, $36a^2b^2$

3. $2x^2 - 4$

4. $4p^2q^3 + 24p^3q - 16p^4q^2$

5. $x(x-3) + 5(x-3)$

6. $p(p^2 - 1) + 4(p^2 - 1)$

Difference of Two Squares (Factor)

7. $x^2 - 36$

8. $75z^2 - 147b^2$

9. $(x - y)^2 - 81$

10. $(2x + 3)^2 - 64$

Trinomials (Factor numbers 11-14, solve number 15-18)

11. $x^2 - 8x + 15$

12. $x^2 + 32 + 12x$

13. $48 + - 16x + x^2$

14. $y^2 + 3y - 18$

15. $(x + 1)(x+2) = 0$

16. $y^2 + 5y - 6 = 0$

17. $3x (4x^2 - 1) = 0$

18. $y^2 + 32y + 256 = 0$

Sums and Differences of Cubes (Factor)

19. $(x^3 - 8)84$

20. $x^3 + 64$

21. $400x^3 - 50$

22. $3x^3 + 81$

Grouping (Factor)

23. $30x^3 + 40x^2 + 3x + 4$

24. $9x^3 + 18x^2 + 7x + 14$

25. $18x^3 + 30x^2 + 3x + 5$

26. $-2x^3 - 4x^2 - 3x - 6$

Evaluate the Discriminant and Number of Solutions

27. $2x^2 + 7x - 15 = 0$

28. $6x^2 = 2x + 7$

29. $8x(x+6) = 0$

30. $5x^2 + 20x = -25$

Factoring Word Problems

31. The area of a rectangle is 72 inches^2. The perimeter of the rectangle is also 36 inches. What are the length and width of this rectangle?

32. The Student Government Association (SGA) is selling chocolate bars to earn money for prom. The total profit (p) is directly related to the amount charged for each candy bar. Profit (p) = $.5x^2$ + 25 x – 150, where x is the number of candy bars sold. What is the fewest number of candy bars that your class must sell to earn $1000 for prom. Assume that the candy bars have no initial cost.

33. The sum of two consecutive integers is 71. Find the smaller of the two integers.

34. Double the product of two consecutive integers is 612. What is the larger integer? Find the smaller of the two integers (one solution is extraneous).

35. If x + y = 7 and x - 7 = 3, what is the value of $(x + y)(x^2 - y^2)$

36. Factor $x^3 - 64$

37. Solve $(x^2 - 1)/(x + 1) = -6$ (Watch for extraneous solutions).

38. What is the least positive integer that is a factor of both 49 and 98?

39. Determine the prime factors of 1024.

40. Explain how to solve a grouping problem.

Algebra Unit 7: Fractions

Notes:

1. To add or subtract fractions, make sure to use a common denominator.

2. Fractions may be multiplied or divided without a common denominator.

3. Polynomials in fractions may only be canceled AFTER factoring.

4. To prepare for this unit, STUDY long and synthetic division.

Adding & Subtracting Like and Unlike Fractions

1. $\frac{3}{8} + \frac{1}{8}$

2. $1\frac{8}{21} - \frac{15}{21}$

3. $\frac{1}{2} + \frac{4}{5}$

4. $\frac{5}{8} - 3\frac{7}{12}$

5. $\frac{2}{3} + \frac{1}{2}$

Multiplying & Dividing Like and Unlike Fractions

6. $\frac{3}{5} * \frac{5}{8}$

7. $\frac{4}{9} * 2$

8. $-3\frac{1}{3} * (-1\frac{1}{5})$

9. $\frac{5}{9} * \frac{12}{45} * \frac{45}{24}$

10. $(\frac{9}{8}) / (\frac{3}{4})$

11. $(\frac{2}{3}) / (\frac{4}{9}) / (\frac{1}{2})$

12. $\left(\frac{5}{8}\right) * \left(\frac{64}{9}\right) / \left(\frac{3}{8}\right)$

Polynomial Fractions

13. $\dfrac{5x^2 + 10x - 15}{25x + 100}$

14. $\dfrac{8x^2 - 4x}{16x^3}$

15. $\dfrac{7x^4}{49x^2 + x^3}$

16. $\dfrac{x^2 - 25}{x^2 + 10x + 25}$

17. $\dfrac{2x}{x^2 + 2x + 1} \div \dfrac{x + 1}{2x^2 + 2x}$

18. $\dfrac{x^2 - 6x - 7}{6x + 30} \div \dfrac{3x + 15}{2x^2 - 50}$

19. $\left(\dfrac{1}{4} + \dfrac{1}{2}\right) \ / \ \left(\dfrac{1}{3} + \dfrac{1}{4}\right)$

20. $\dfrac{4\frac{1}{2} + 1\frac{2}{3}}{2\frac{1}{4} - 1\frac{3}{8}}$

Practice Problems

21. $x = (2y)/3$
    $y = (3z)/5$
    Find $\dfrac{x}{z}$

22. $\dfrac{x}{4} + \dfrac{7}{4} = \dfrac{-3}{x}$

23. What fraction of 6 hours is 180 seconds?

24. If d and e are positive numbers and $\dfrac{de}{a-e} = 1$, what does $e = ?$

25. Given $vz \neq 0, z = \dfrac{1}{v}$, what does $(1-v)/(1-z) = ?$

26. Of 300 students in a class, ¼ of the students earned an A for the last test, ⅓ of the students earned a B and the rest earned a C. How many students earned a C for the exam?

27. Four identically sized candy jars have candy in each of them. Jar A is ¼ full, Jar B is ½ full, Jar C is ⅘ full and Jar D is empty. If the candy were redistributed equally among all four jars, what fractional part of each jar would be filled.

28. Jonathan ordered a pizza and ate 2 of the eight slices and divided the rest equally among three friends. How many slices did each friend receive?

29. Rearrange this fraction into fractions with common denominators: $\frac{(4x+6)}{(3x+3)} + 5$

30. What are all possible solutions (excluding extraneous solutions) for $x/(x-2) = (5x)/2$?

Algebra Unit 8: Linear Equations and Lines

Notes:

1. Equation of a vertical line: x = number, slope is undefined

2. Equation of a horizontal line: y = number, slope = 0

3. Standard equation of a line: $Ax + By = C$

4. Slope intercept form of a line: $y = mx + b$

5. Slope is rise/run or $(y_2 - y_1) / (x_2 - x_1)$

6. Slope = m

7. Y-intercept = b

8. Point slope formula of a line: $y - y_1 = m(x - x_1)$

9. To find x-intercept, set y to 0.

10. To find y-intercept, set x to 0.

11. Parallel lines have the same slope

12. Perpendicular lines have the opposite sign reciprocal slope

Practice Problems

1. What is the slope of the line that passes through (-2, 1) and (2, -5)?

2. What is the equation of the line above?

3. What is the slope of the line in the equation $7x = 4y + 2$

4. Name the slope and the y-intercept of of the following line: $3y - 2x = -1$

5. In the xy plane, line l has a y-intercept of -13 and is perpendicular to the line with equation $y = -\frac{2}{3}$ x. If the point (10, b) is on line l, what is the value of b?

6. What is the equation of the line containing the points (1,3) and (2,4)?

7. What is the slope of the following line: $x = 7y + 14$?

8. What is the equation of the line with the following points?
   (a, 0), (3a, -a), (5a, -2a)

9. What is the equation of the line below?

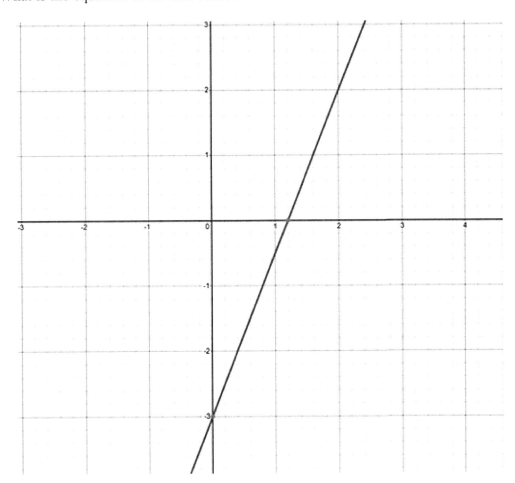

10.

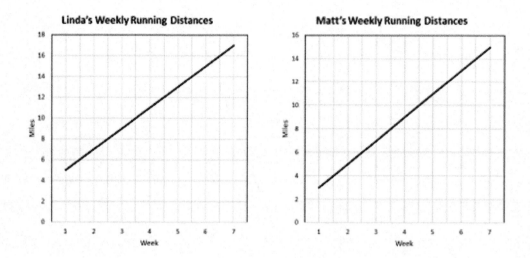

The two graphs above show the number of miles that Matt and Linda ran each week for seven weeks. What is the equation of the lines for each runner? How many more miles did Linda run each week?

11. The graph below shows the relationship between the height and the volume of two grain silos. The base diameter of MRTB's silo is 20 feet and the base diameter of Mr. Ross' silo is 50 feet. How tall is MRTB's silo and how tall is Mr. Ross' silo? How much taller is Mr. Ross' silo than MRTB's silo?

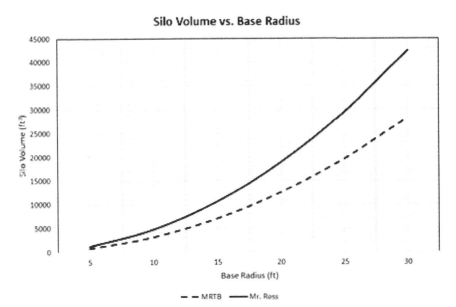

12.

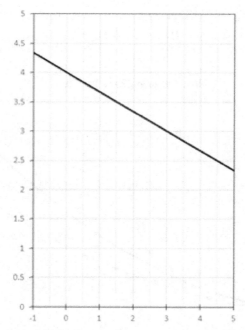

The graph of a linear function (line a) is shown in the xy-plane above. The graph of line b is perpendicular to line a and passes through the point (2, 4). What is the value of b(0)?

13.

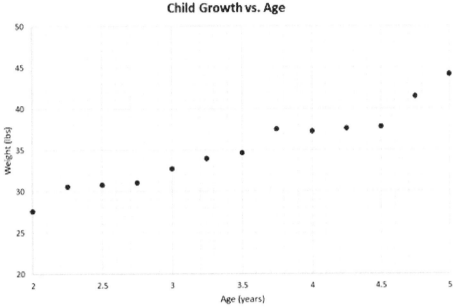

Child Growth vs. Age

[Calculator] The scatterplot above shows the growth of a child from two to five years. What is the line of best fit for the scatter plot?

14. Professional Tutoring purchased a Mercedes G-Wagon for company use for the cost of $180,000. If the car depreciates by the same amount each year so that the car is worth $40,000 after ten years, what is the linear equation of the depreciation over 10 years?

15. A computer with the cost of $1300 is to be purchased over time with an initial down payment of $300 and a monthly payment of $50. How many months will it take Wilbur to pay off the computer?

16. Verson Telephone Company charges an initial fee of $150 and $60 per month for phone usage. How much will the phone cost after two-and-a-half years?

17. Netflax charges a $25 monthly fee plus $5 for each movie rented. How much will it cost for a year-long membership with six rentals per month?

18. If a boat club charges $1500 for the first week-long cruise and $1200 for each additional week, write the linear equation that represents the total cost to date by week.

19. A plumber charges $125 per hour with a $200 visit charge. How much would a five-hour visit cost? Solve for the visit cost and write a linear equation.

20. Find the equations of the vertical and horizontal lines that pass through (-5, 6).

Algebra Unit 9:
Graphing Linear, Quadratic, Cubic and Absolute Value Equations

Notes:

1. Linear Equations have the following forms and rules.

   $m =$ slope and $b = y$ intercept

   a. Standard: $ax + by = c$

   b. Slope Intercept: $y = mx + b$

   c. Point slope: $(y - y_1) = m(x - x_1)$

   d. Slope may be calculated using the following function: $(y_2 - y_1)/(x_2 - x_1)$

   e. Linear equations with identical slopes are parallel and never meet. Therefore, they have no solution.

   f. Linear equations with opposite (sign), reciprocal slopes are perpendicular and meet in exactly one point.

2. Quadratic Equations have the following forms

   a. Standard: $ax^2 + bx + c$

   b. Vertex: $a(x - h)^2 + k$, where (h, k) is the vertex

   c. Line of Symmetry: Based on standard form: $x = -b/(2a)$

   d. Vertex: L.O.S. x value, y value is evaluated by plugging x into the original standard form equation

   e. Minimum/Maximum: Vertex values

   f. $y = +x^2$ opens up. $y = -x^2$ opens down. $x = y^2$ opens right, $x = -y^2$ opens left

3. Equations with exponents of three or greater will generally be graphed on a calculator.

4. All graphs have parent functions.

   a. Linear: $y = x$

   b. Quadratic: $y = x^2$

   c. Cubic, etc.: $y = x^3$

5. All graphs transforms transform according to the following:

   1) (x) - a: shifts a units down

   2) $(x) + a$: shifts a units up

3) $(x - a)$: shifts a units right (opposite of its sign)

4) $(x + a)$: shifts a units left (opposite of its sign)

5) $-(x)$: flips over the x axis

6) $y = a(x)$: $a > 1$, vertical stretch

7) $y = a(x)$: $0 < a < 1$, compression

8) $x \geq$ Shades above/inside the graphing lines, solid inequality line

9) $x \leq$ Shades below the graphing lines, solid inequality line

10) $x >$ or $x <$ Dotted line

6. The zeroes of functions are the x intercepts. To find the x intercepts, set $y = 0$, To find the y intercepts, set $x = 0$

7. Domain = all x values. Range = all y values

8. Cubic and equations of higher degrees will generally allow use of a calculator. If the questions refer to simple transformations, you will be expected to answer without a calculator.

9.

   a. Absolute value is indicated by straight brackets around a number $|x|$. It is defined as the distance a number is from 0 on a number line. The absolute value of $+7$ and -7 is the same (7).

   b. Absolute value may also be graphed on the coordinate plane.

   The parent graph is $|x| = 0$

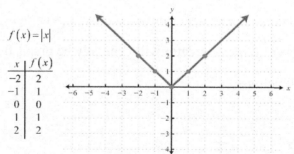

   c. General Form of an Absolute Value Equation/Function

$$Y = a|x - h| + k$$

   $a =$ stretch or compression factor. Vertex is (h, k), the axis of symmetry is $x = h$

10. Make yourself familiar with piecewise functions.

Linear Equation Practice Problems:

Identify the slope, x intercept and y intercept AND graph the equation on the coordinate plane.

1. (3, 2) and (-1, -1)

   Slope:

   Equation:

   X intercept:

   Y intercept:

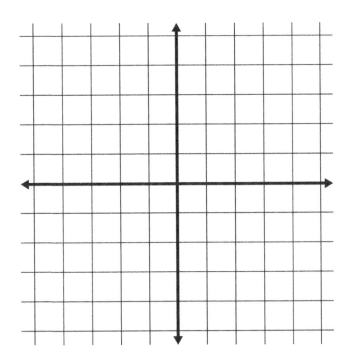

2. (-1, 0) and (0, -1)

Slope:

Equation:

X intercept:

Y intercept:

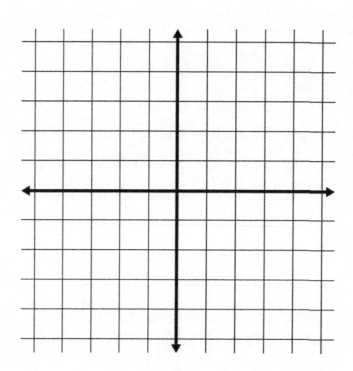

Quadratic Equation Practice Problems

3. $y = x^2 - 2x - 3$

Identify the vertex, the axis of symmetry, the maximum or minimum value, the range and domain of each quadratic equation below. Graph the equation on the coordinate plane.

Vertex:

Axis of Symmetry:

Minimum/Maximum:

Range:

Domain:

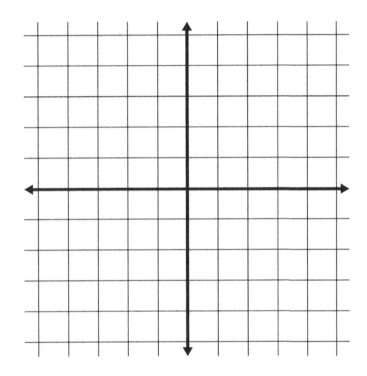

4. $y = x^2 - 2x + 1$

Identify the vertex, the axis of symmetry, the maximum or minimum value, the range and domain of each quadratic equation below. Graph the equation on the coordinate plane.

Vertex:

Axis of Symmetry:

Minimum/Maximum:

Range:

Domain:

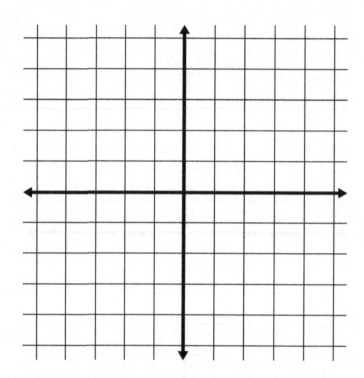

5. Solve, graph and shade the following inequality: $|x - 3| > 2$

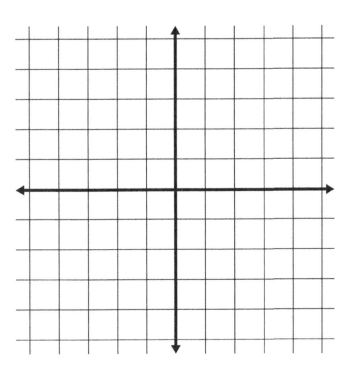

6. Solve, graph and shade the following inequality: $|2x + 6| \leq 8$

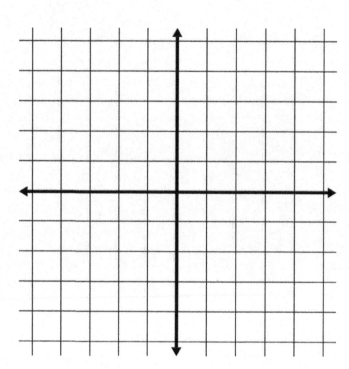

Linear and Quadratic Equation Word Problems

7. Suppose you are doing a 5000-piece puzzle. You have already placed 175 pieces. Every minute you place 10 more pieces.

   a. Write an equation in slope-intercept form to model the number of pieces placed. Graph the equation.

   b. After 50 more minutes, how many pieces will you have placed?

8. Suppose you have a $5-off coupon at a fabric store. You buy fabric that costs $7.50 per yard. Write an equation that models the total amount of money, y, you pay if you buy x yards of fabric. What is the graph of the equation?

9. The temperature at sunrise is 65°F. Each hour during the day, the temperature rises 5°F. Write an equation that models the temperature y, in degrees Fahrenheit, after x hours during the day. What is the graph of the equation?

10. A sailboat begins a voyage with 145-lbs of food. The crew plans to eat a total of 15-lbs of food per day.

    a. Write an equation in slope-intercept form relating the remaining food supply y to the number of days x.

    b. Graph your equation.

    c. The crew plans to have 25-lbs of food remaining when they end their voyage. How many days does the crew expect their voyage to last?

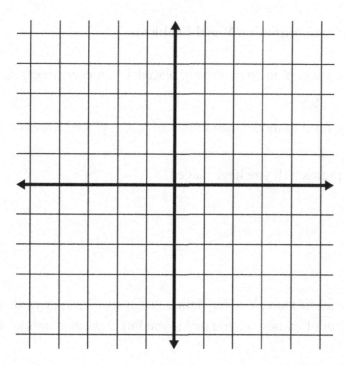

11. A student government association wants to maximize profit by selling mulch. The earnings can be modeled with the equation: $R = -2.5p^2 + 100p$, where p is the price in dollars per bag of mulch. What price will earn the students the greatest gross profit?

12. A penny dropped from the Washington Monument (555 feet tall) will fall in the model: $h = -16t^2 + 555$, where t is seconds. How long will it take the penny to hit the ground?

13. On Mars, objects fall much more slowly than they do on earth. How long would a penny take to fall from the same height of 555 feet according to the model, $h = -6t^2 + 555$, where t is seconds.

14. From 1990 through 2010, the number of iPhones sold can be approximated by the equation $.5c^2 - 5c + 7.8$ with the year $1990 = 0$. How many phones were sold in 2000 and in 2010?

15. If the graph of $y = x^2 + 5x + 6$ is graphed, the graph crosses the y-axis at the point $(0,k)$. What is the value of k?

16. In the xy-plane, a line and quadratic equation cross at exactly one point. If the equation of the parabola is $y = -x^2 + 5x + 0$ and the equation of the line is $y = c$, what is the value of c?

17. In the xy-plane, the graph of $y = x^2 + 5x + 6$ has exactly two x-intercepts. What are they and what is the distance between them?

18. $Y = -(x - 4)^2 + b$. In this equation, b is a constant. What is the value of the minimum or maximum?

19. In the xy-plane, the following quadratic crosses the x axis at exactly two points $(a, 0)$ and $(b, 0)$. What is the equation of this quadratic in factored form and standard form?

20. The equation $24x^2 + 2x = 16$ has exactly two solutions. What is the difference between the two solutions?

Algebra Unit 10. Systems of Equations

Notes:

There are four methods to solve systems of equations:

1. Substitution

2. Linear Combination

3. Graphing

4. Matrices

With linear systems of one or two degrees (exponent is 1 or 2), there are 1, 0 or infinite solutions:

1. <u>One solution</u>: The lines cross at a single point on the graph.

2. <u>No solution</u>: The lines are parallel; they never cross. The slopes (m) are the same and the y-intercepts (b) are different.

3. <u>Infinite solutions</u>: The lines are the same. The slopes and the y-intercepts are the same.

Note: These rules follow the discriminant rules (under notes in Chapter 5)

Determine if the ordered pair is a solution of the system.

1. (4, -2)

   $2x - 4y = 6$
   $-x + 3y = 14$

2. $(\frac{2}{3}, 0)$

   $-3x + 2y = 2$
   $3x + 2y = -2$

Solve with substitution

3. $x - 4y = 20$
   $2x + 5y = 1$

4. $x + 3y = -2$
   $-3x + y = 6$

Solve with linear combination/elimination

5. $9x - 5y = -30$
   $x + 5y = 18$

6. $-x + y = -14$
   $-2x + 3y = 6$

Graph the following equations and state the solution.

7. $2x + y = 4$
   $x - y = 2$

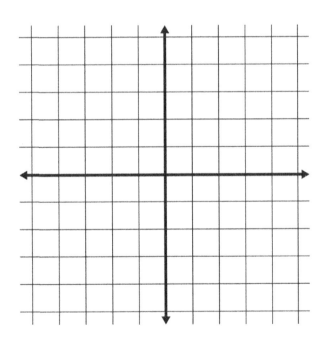

8. $x + y = 4$
    $x + y = 2$

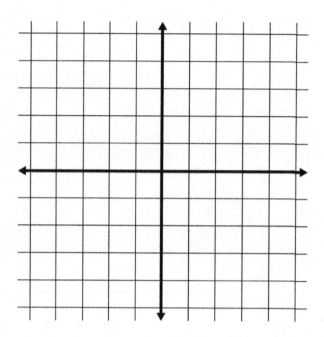

9. If: $3y - 4x = 5$
    $2y - 3x = 10$
    What is the value of $y - x$?

10. Find the value of $a - b$, if
    $-2a - 5b = -15$ and
    $3a + 4b = 19$

11. Find the value of 3a - 2b, if

$12 = 4a - 3b$ and

$7a = 5b - 2$

12. Tickets for a concert cost $10 each if you order them online, but you must pay a service charge of $8 per order. The tickets are $12 each if you buy them at the door on the night of the concert.

   a. Write a system of equations to model the situation. Let *c* be the total cost. Let *t* be the number of tickets.

   b. Graph the equation and find the intersection point. What does this point represent?

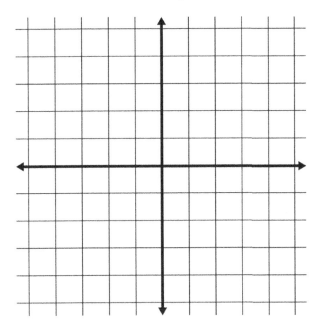

13. The number of right-handed students in a math class is nine times the number of left-handed students. The total number of students in the class is 30. How many right-handed students are in the class? How many left-handed students are in the class?

14. A rocket is launched from the Robinson launching field. It follows the path of $y = -x^2 + 5x$. At the same time, an arrow is shot in a linear path of $y = x + 6$. At what point do the rocket and arrow intersect? Solve algebraically and graph.

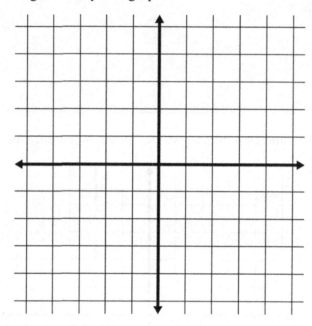

15. The price of AT&S stock can be modeled by the equation $y = .66x^2 - 10x + 25$. The price of Nerdizon stock has increased at a steady linear path of $y = 5x + 15$. When do the two stocks equal each other?

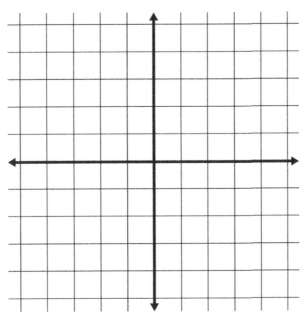

16. Alexander is bungee jumping. His jump can be modeled by the equation $h = -4.9t^2 + t + 360$. The bungee's resistance takes effect after several seconds which can be modeled at $h = -4t + 100$. After how many seconds did the bungee begin to pull back?

17. Graph and shade the following equations:

a) $y \leq x + 2$
b) $2x + 3y \geq 6$

18. If $2x + 4y = 14$ and $4x + 5y = 25$, what does $2x + 3y$ equal?

19. If a delivery truck transports 100-pound packages and 120-pound packages and the truck must carry at least 10 packages and the total weight of the packages cannot exceed 1400 pounds, what is the maximum number of 120-pound packages that the truck can transport?

20. The system $3x - 2y = 48$ and $ax - by = 9$ have no solutions. If a and b are constants, what is the value of a/b?

21. The sum of two positive integers is 151. The smaller number is 19 more than the square root of the greater number. What is the value of each number?

Mastery Unit B

1. Simplify $\dfrac{2}{\frac{1}{d} - \frac{1}{e}}$

2. In a bowl of M & M candies, $\frac{1}{4}$ are green, $\frac{1}{3}$ are red, $\frac{1}{6}$ are yellow and $\frac{1}{12}$ are brown, what fractional part remains?

3. When a polynomial is divided by $(x - 5)$, the quotient is $5x^2 + 3x + 12$ with remainder 7. Find the polynomial.

4. If the polynomial $x^3 + 6x^2 + 13x + 6$ expresses the volume, in cubic inches, of a box, and the width is $(x + 1)$ inches and the height is (x - 2), what is the depth of the box?

5. Solve the linear system using substitution or linear combination.

   $3x - y = 7$
   $2x + 3y = 1$

6. You buy a CD player for $150 and start to purchase CD's at $6.50 each. At what point will you have spent more on cd's than on the CD player?

7. Liam is considering two phone plans. Plan A offers a flat rate of $216 per month for unlimited calls, texting and data. Plan B offers a plan dependent on use. Calls and texting cost $50 per month. Phone rental is $37 per month. Data usage costs $17 per month per 2 GB of use. At what point are the two plans equal in cost.?

8. Find the solution of $y = x^2 - 6x + 8$ and $y = 3x + 2$. Graph the solution.

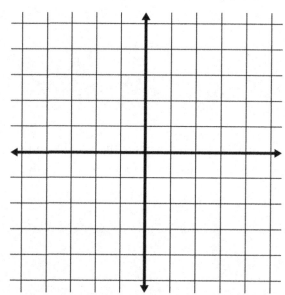

9. How many times do the following equations intersect?

   $y = x^2 + 4$ and $y = 2$

10. Find the linear inequality that has a slope of $\frac{1}{3}$ and a y-intercept of -2. The area above the solid line is shaded. What inequality should you write?

11. Meredith has $125,000 saved for medical school. If she will need to complete six years of medical school at a cost of $50,000 per year, how much will she have to borrow each year on average to have enough to finance her entire program?

12. Given the points (-7, 5) and (-5, -7), find the following:

Equation:

X intercept:

Y intercept:

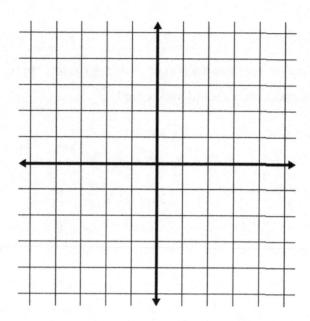

13. Given the points (1, 1) and (-1, -1), find the following:

Equation:

X intercept:

Y intercept:

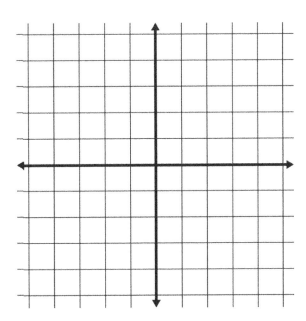

14. Solve: $7 - |2x + 6| - y = 4$

Algebraic work:

Transformation:

Stretch/Compression

X intercept:

Y intercept:

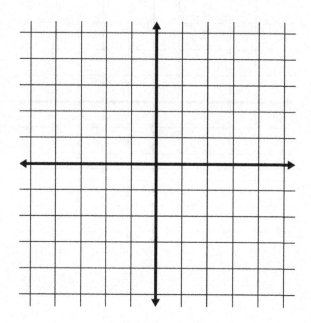

15. $-3x + y = 2$

    $ax + 2y = 4$

    In the system of equations above, a is a constant. For what value does the system have infinite solutions?

16. $4x - 2y = 16$

    $2x + 4y = 8$

    What is the value of $x + y$?

17. $24x - 15y = 3$

    $16x + 5y = -13$

    What is the point of intersection of the linear system above?

18. $.5x + 2.5y = 15$

    $.75x + 12.5y = 8$

    What is the value of $250x + 300y$?

19. What is the value of $|-4 + 8| - |-3 + 6|$

20. Transform the graph six units down and five units to the left:

$f(x) = x^2$

Algebra Unit 11: Proportions, Ratios, Percentages

Notes:

1. Ratios and proportions may be written in three ways:

   $\frac{x}{y}$ $x : y$ x is to y

2. Percentages represent a proportion, a part to a whole, and based on 100.

3. To change from a fraction to a percent:

   a) Divide to a decimal

   b) Multiply by 100

   $$\text{e.g.:} \quad \frac{5}{8} = 0.625$$
   $$.625 * 100 = 62.5\%$$

4. To set up the percentage equation:

   a) $\dfrac{is}{of} = \dfrac{\%}{100}$ or $\dfrac{part}{whole} = \dfrac{\%}{100}$

   b) Cross-multiply and solve.

Set a ratio/fraction and simplify

1. 11 out of 121

2. 18 out of 27

3. 65 out of 200

4. 118 out of 354

Set as a unit rate

5. 364 miles on 9.2 gallons

6. $210 for 15 tickets

7. 18 inches of snow in 4 hours

8. $67,000 prize for 100 people

Solve for the variable

9. $\dfrac{3}{7} = \dfrac{m}{49}$

10. $\dfrac{6}{9.6} = \dfrac{x}{1.6}$

11. $\dfrac{r}{3} = \dfrac{8}{15}$

12. $\dfrac{7}{16} = \dfrac{x}{4.8}$

Express each fraction as a percent

13. $\frac{31}{100}$

14. $\frac{3}{8}$

15. $\frac{6}{5}$

16. $\frac{7}{3}$

Solve

17. 40% of 60

18. 60% of 40

19. 7.5% of 80

20. 16 is what percent of 40?

21. 37 is what percent of 296?

22. $\frac{1}{2}$ is what percent of 8?

23. 28 is 20% of what number?

24. 19 is what percent of 76?

25. 16 is 40% of what number?

Word Problems

26. If 10 fraternity members can mow the UVA lawn in twelve hours, how long would it take 6 fraternity members?

27. Jose is purchasing 4 dress shirts that cost $28 each and 2 pairs of pants that cost $38 each. The items are all on sale for 35% off. How much money will Jose save by purchasing them on sale instead of at full price?

28. If the United States recycles about 18% of the glass bottles and jars in the United States and the total number of glass vessels on any given day is 14,709,741, how many are recycled daily? How many are not recycled?

29. You bought a pair of shoes for $25 and your friend bought the same pair for $30, what percentage more did your friend pay?

30. If a gold ring is discounted 27% and its discounted price is $550, what was its original price?

Algebra Unit 12: Functions

Notes:

Relation: A set of ordered pairs (x, y).

Inputs: x values, also called domain.

Outputs: y values, also called range.

Function: A special type of relationship between two values in which each input value corresponds to exactly one output value. If two or more ordered pairs have the same x value, the relation is not a function. Functions must pass the vertical line test.

Function Notation: A "normal" equation is written in standard from:

$$x + y = 5 \quad \text{or} \quad y = -x + 5$$

Written in function notation: $f(x) = -x + 5$

To Solve a Function: A function will be written in the following format: $f(x) = x - 9$

Find the indicated value of f(3): $f(x) = x - 9$.

$$f(3) = 3 - 9$$

$$f(3) = -6$$

Function Operations: $f(x) = 3x$ and $g(x) = x - 5$

Addition: $f(x) + g(x) = 3x + (x - 5) = 4x - 5$

Subtraction: $f(x) - g(x) = 3x - (x - 5) = 3x - x + 5 = 2x + 5$

Multiplication: $f(x) * g(x) = 3x * (x - 5) = 3x^2 - 15x$

Division: $f(x) \div g(x) = (3x)/(x - 5)$

Composition of Two Functions:

$f(x) = 4x + 2$ and $g(x) = x - 3$ Find $f(g(x))$

Steps: 1)   Substitute: $f(g(x)) = f(x - 3)$

                     2)   Plug g(x) into f(x): $4(x - 3) + 2$

$$4x - 12 + 2$$

$$4x - 10 = f(g(x))$$

Inverse of Functions:

Written as $f(x)^{-1}$: the inverse of $f(x) = 4x + 2$

Steps:

1) Rewrite: $y = 4x + 2$

2) Change x and y: $x = 4y + 2$

3) Solve for y: $y = \frac{1}{4}x - \frac{1}{2}$

Solve

1. Find the domain and range: $\{(1,5),(-2,8),(0,4),(-1,5),(2,8)\}$

2. Is the relation in #1 a function? Why or why not?

3. Find the domain and range: $\{(4,1),(7,2),(7,-2),(3,0),(4,-1)\}$

4. Is the relation in #3 a function? Why or why not?

5. Given $f(x) = 10x + 2$, find the value of $f(-1)$.

6. Given $f(x) = -x^2 - 4x + 3$, find the value of $f(10)$.

Given f(x) = 2x − 4 and g(x) = x − 1, solve for h(x)

7. h(x) = f(x) + g(x)

8. h(x) = f(x) − g(x)

9. h(x) = f(x) − 3g(x)

10. h(x) = $\frac{1}{2}$f(x) + 2g(x)

11. h(x) = f(x) * g(x)

12. $h(x) = f(x) \div g(x)$

13. $h(x) = f(g(x))$

14. $h(x) = g(f(x))$

Find the inverses of the following functions

15. $f(x) = 11x + 22$

16. $f(x) = \frac{1}{2}(x - 10)$

17. $f(x) = x^2 - 1$

18. $f(x) = (15x + 6)/(x + 2)$

SAT & ACT Exam Problems

19. $f(x) = (x + 3)/2$ What is the value of $f(-1)$

20. $f(x) = 4x^2 - 6(3x + 2)$. What is the value of $f(-3)$

21. $f(x) = 3^x$. What is the value of $f(3) - f(2)$?

22. The number of citizens in Berkeley Heights at the beginning of each year can be modeled by the equation $f(x) = 3(2^x)$ where 3 represents tens of thousands and x represents the number of years after 2000. For example, $x = 1$ represents the year 2001 and so on. According to this model, how many people lived in Berkeley Heights in 2007?

23. What is the maximum value of the function $f(x) = -5x^2 - 6$

24. If $f(x) = 5x^2 - 3$ and the $f(x + a) = 5x^2 + 30x + 42$, what is the value of a?

25. Given that $f(x) = (x^2 - 4)$ and $g(x) = x + 3$, what is the value of $f(g(0))$?

Algebra Unit 13: Exponential Growth and Decay

Notes:

1. Exponential growth has a base greater than 1.0 (ex. 2^x)

2. Exponential decay has a base less than 1.0 (ex. 0.85^x)

3. Simple Interest/Growth/Decay: $A = P(1 + rt)$
   $A =$ future value, $P =$ principal value, $r =$ rate, $t =$ time

4. Compound Interest: $A = P(1 + \frac{r}{n})^{nt}$ $A =$ future value, $P =$ principal value, $r =$ rate, $n =$ number of times the interest compounds per year, $t =$ time in years.

5. Continuous Interest: $A = Pe^{rt}$ $A =$ future value, $P =$ Principal, $e =$ integral that we use for continuous growth and decay; e is a function on your calculator. $R = \%$ rate, $t =$ time.

Word Problems

Given that Jenny deposited $2000 in a bank account and let it grow for ten years with an 8% compounded interest rate. How much interest did she earn with the following compounding periods?

1. Annual

2. Quarterly

3. Monthly

4. Daily

5. Continuous

Given a 30 year deposit with a total of $242,000 with a 7% interest rate. How much interest did Natha earn with the following compounding periods?

6. Annual

7. Quarterly

8. Monthly

9. Daily

10. Continuous

11. Dr. G. purchases a car for $52,000. If the car loses 15% of its value annually, how much is the car worth after 4 years?

Julia put $122,000 into the stock market in 2015. The stocks lost money over a five-year period at the rate of 7.9%. Find the values at:

12. 1 year

13. 3 years

14. 5 years

15. A family sells a car to a dealership for 60% less than they paid for it. They paid $9000 for the car. For what price did they sell the car?

16. Addison forms a new company with 30 employees and sets a goal of doubling her employees every year. If f(e) is the number of employees e years after Addison launched her company, best describe the function:

    a) The function is a decreasing linear function.

    b) The function is an increasing linear function.

    c) The function is a decreasing exponential function.

    d) The function is an increasing exponential function.

17. Jeremy modeled the growth of bacteria in a petri dish over 24 hours. At the beginning there were 1500 bacteria. He estimated a 20% increase in the number of bacteria per minute. Write a function that models the number of bacteria t minutes after Jeremy began measuring.

18. Jorge purchased gold coins that had a value of $500. He estimated that his coins would increase by 18% each year. The estimated value of the coins three years after purchase can be represented by the expressions 500a, where a is a constant. What is the value of a?

19. In 2010, the average restaurant server earned $2.10 per hour (outside of tips). In 2020, federal law required the restaurant industry to increase the hourly rate to $2.50 per hour. During the same time period, the cost of living increased by 4.7 percent. How much would servers' salaries have to have increased over that same ten-year period to keep up with inflation?

20. Elephant embryos growth is exponential at $f(t)=.250 * 1.35^t$ where $f(t)$ is the total weight in milligrams and t is the age of the embryo in days. How much will an elephant embryo weigh at 50 days of gestation?

Algebra Unit 14: Imaginary Numbers

Notes:

For many students, who have always worked with real numbers, imaginary numbers are just incomprehensible! So what is an imaginary number? The square root of –1 is the basic unit of imaginary numbers, represented by i. $i = \sqrt{-1}$

The four basic math functions (addition, subtraction, multiplication and division) follow the basic rules of algebra that variables follow:

1. Different forms of i: Imaginary numbers may be represented in three ways:

    a) i

    b) $\sqrt{-1}$

    c) $i\sqrt{1}$ (the negative sign may be removed from the radical symbol and represented by an i in front of the radical sign). For example, $\sqrt{-6}$ may be represented by $i\sqrt{6}$.

2. Standard Form Equation: The standard form of an imaginary number equation is $a \pm bi$

3. Conjugate: The conjugate of the standard form of an imaginary number equation is also $a \pm bi$. The conjugate uses the opposite sign. For example, for the standard equation $a + bi$, the conjugate is $a - bi$.

4. Addition/Subtraction: Add or subtract coefficients. Examples:

    a) $i + 6i = 7i$

    b) $15i + 7i + 2 = 22i + 2$

    c) $46i - 52i + 9i = 3i$

    d) $-7 - 9 + 33i - 65i = -16 - 32i$

5. Multiplication/Division: Like all variables, imaginary numbers add or subtract exponents when like variables are multiplied or divided. As with variables, the coefficients multiply or divide separately from the variables' interactions. Examples:

    a) $6i * 7i = 42i^2$

    b) $5 * 8i * 2i^3 = 80i^4$

    c) $(32i^3)/(8i) = 4i$

    d) $(45i^6)/9i^9 = 5i^{-3}$ or $5/i^3$

6. Exponential Forms: The i, or basic unit of imaginary numbers, may grow exponentially into infinity. The ultimate value of the unit will also come down to four values:

$$i^1 = \sqrt{-1}$$
$$i^2 = -1$$
$$i^3 = -i$$
$$i^4 = 1$$

This pattern will repeat indefinitely. While i values may be computed on a calculator, students may also derive them through simple division. The steps include

a) Divide the imaginary number's exponent by 4. Ignore the coefficient.

b) The remainder will indicate what form of i will be left. Remainders may be decimals if using a calculator numbers 1-4 if using long division.

o A remainder of 1 or .25 will yield a value of i or $\sqrt{-1}$

o A remainder of 2 or .5 will yield a value of i^2 or -1

o A remainder of 3 or .75 will yield a value of i^3 or $-i$ or $-\sqrt{-1}$

o A remainder of 4 or 0.0 will yield a value of i^4 or 1

7. Negative Exponents: Imaginary numbers may be raised to negative exponents as well as to positive exponents as outlined above. When an imaginary number is raised to a negative exponent, the imaginary number will drop to the denominator of the fraction.

8. Rationalizing: Radicals, of any type, may NOT occur in the denominator of a fraction. Therefore, radicals which appear in the denominator of a fraction must be multiplied out to reach a single positive value or a polynomial with NO radicals. You will either multiply by i raised to an exponent (between 1 and 3) or by the conjugate of the binomial.

Practice Problems

1. $\sqrt{-144x} =$

2. $\sqrt{-254} =$

3. Find the conjugate of $a + bi$

4. Find the conjugate of $5 - 6i$

5. $(5 + 6i) + (6 - 3i) =$

6. $(1 + 5i) - (3 - 2i) =$

7. $\sqrt{-5} * \sqrt{7} =$

8. $\sqrt{9} * \sqrt{-9} =$

9. $i^{66} =$

10. $i^6 * i^9 =$

11. $5i^5 * 7i^8 =$

12. $98i^6 * (1/14)i^2 =$

13. $75i^9/25i^8 =$

14. $144i^6/12i^4 =$

15. $(36 + 6i)/(6 + i) =$

16. $72/(6 * \sqrt{-7}) =$

17. $1/(4i^{-1}) =$

18. $(24i^{-5}) =$

19. $15i^{-2} =$

20. $5/(6 + i^3) =$

21. $(x^3 + 3x^2 + 4x + 12)/(x + 2i) =$

22. $(x^2 + 9)/(x + 3i) =$

23. $(x - 6i)^{-1} =$

24. What is the quotient of $\frac{5-2i}{3+4i}$?

25. Rewrite the expression $(8 - 5i)^2$ in the form of $a + bi$.

26. $6x^2 - 5i^2 = 2x^2 - i^2$

27. $(5 + 5i) - 2i^2(1 + 3i) =$

28. $4i[3i(2 + i) - (3 - 9i)] =$

29. $7x^2 - 5 - 2x = 8x^2 + 5$

30. $-3x^2 - 5x - 3 =$

Algebra Unit 15: Basic Statistics: Probability: Basic, Conditional, Independent, and Dependent. Permutations and Combinations, Fundamental Counting Principal

Define

1. Mean/Average: _____

2. Mode: _____

3. Median: _____

4. Range: _____

5. I'quartile Range: _____

6. Scatter Plot: _____

7. Correlation: _____

8. Probability: _____

9. Basic Prob: _____

10. Conditional Prob.: _____

11. Independent Prob.: _____

12. Dependent Prob.: _____

13. Fund. Counting Prin.: _____

Notes:

1. Mean/Average

    a. Arithmetic: the sum of n numbers divided by n

        i. $\dfrac{a_1 + a_2 + \cdots + a_n}{n}$

    b. Geometric: the nth root of a product of n numbers

        i. $\sqrt[n]{a_1 a_2 \cdots a_n}$

    c. Since the mean considers all values in a dataset, it is susceptible to influence by outliers.

2. Mode

    a. The most common data value. If no one value occurs the most, then the mode is none.

3. Median

    a. The center value of an ordered dataset. If the dataset has an even number of values, the median is the average of the two center values.

4. Percentile

    a. The kth percentile is the value at or below which k percent of the data values fall.

        i. The data must be ordered from lowest to highest

        ii. There are several different ways to calculate percentiles. Focus on using them to find quartiles, discussed below.

5. Quartile

    a. A quartile is a quarter of a dataset. The quartiles are demarcated by the 25th, 50th, and 75th percentiles of a dataset. These are called the first (Q_1), second (Q_2), and third (Q_3) quartiles, respectively.

    b. Find the quartile values by splitting the data set into four equal parts.

        i. Find the median. This is Q_3.

        ii. Divide in half the datasets on both sides of the median. If there is no central value, find the average between the two most central values. Essentially, this is like finding the median of both the top and bottom halves of the dataset. These will be your Q_1 and Q_3.

    c. Using an example dataset: [1, 2, 3, 4, 5, 6, 7, 8, 9, 10, 11, 12]

        i. Q_1 is 3.5

        ii. Q_2 is equivalent to the median and is 6.5

      iii.   Q3 is 9.5

6. Interquartile Range

    a. The central 50% of values.

    b. IQR = Q3 - Q1

    c. From the above dataset, the IQR would be 9.5 - 3.5 = 6.

7. Fundamental Counting Principle

    a. A method of determining the number of possible outcomes in a probability problem.

    b. Often, a probability problem can be broken into stages. The FCP determines the number of possible outcomes by finding the product of the number of possibilities within each stage.

    c. For example, to find the number of possible ways an ice cream can be served, FCP says to multiply the types of ice cream, by the drizzle flavors, by sprinkle type. If there are 5 flavors of ice cream, three drizzle flavors, and 10 sprinkle types, then there are $5 \times 10 \times 3 = 150$ possible ways to serve that ice cream.

8. Independent probability

    a. Probability problems can be simplified if it is assumed that the variables involved are independent of each other.

    b. Independent variables do not influence each other.

    c. For example, if the occurrence of event A increased the likelihood of event B occurring, then A and B would not be independent.

    d. If variables are independent and equally likely to occur, the probability of X occurring can be found by dividing the number of ways X can occur by the total number of possibilities (i.e. including possibilities where X does not occur).

    e. For example, in the ice cream example above, the probability that one ice cream flavor out of five total options will be chosen is ⅕ (20%) assuming that each flavor is equally likely to be chosen and independent of other variables.

9. AND Probability

    a. To determine the probability that an event A *and* an event B will occur, find the product of their respective probabilities. Must assume that events A and B are independent.

    b. For example, using the ice cream problem above, to find the probability that the ice cream will be vanilla with chocolate drizzle, state that this is equivalent to the probability of vanilla multiplied by the probability of chocolate drizzle. If all possibilities are equally likely, and each flavor of ice cream and drizzle is different, then this results in $\frac{1}{5} \times \frac{1}{3} = \frac{1}{15}$ or 6.7%.

10. OR Probability

    a. To determine the probability that an event A *or* an event B will occur, find the sum of their respective probabilities. Must assume that events A and B are independent and mutually exclusive. Mutually exclusive means that both events cannot occur simultaneously.

11. Correlation

    a. Two variables are correlated if there is an observed relationship between them. Often a correlation can be seen on a scatter plot.

    b. On a scatter plot, one variable is displayed on the horizontal axis and another is on the vertical axis.

    c. A line of best fit can be plotted to determine the relationship. A calculator is usually used to find the line of best fit.

        i. A line of best fit is a line that minimizes the distance between the line and all data points.

        ii. If the line of best fit has a positive slope, this is a *positive* relationship because as variable X increases, so does variable Y.

        iii. If the line of best fit has a negative slope, this is a *negative* relationship because as variable X increases, variable Y decreases.

        iv. If the line of best fit has a zero slope, there is no relationship because as variable X increases, variable Y is unaffected.

Solve

1. Find the arithmetic mean, mode and median of the following data:

   130, 155, 148, 184, and 172

   Mean:

   Mode:

   Median:

2. Find the arithmetic mean, mode and median of the following data:

   25, 98, 30, 45, 36, 25, and 62

   Mean:

   Mode:

   Median:

3. The average of $2x - 1$, 4, 6, 12 and 13 is 9. What is the value of x?

4. What is the average of: x, $x - 3$, $2x - 5$, $2x + 2$ and $1 - x$?

5. The mean of x and y is 4. If $x = 5y$, what is y?

6. What number must be added to 6, 16, and 8 to have an average of 13?

7. After a fourth quiz, Kristin's English grade dropped from 98 to 95, what was her fourth quiz grade?

8. Kelly earned a 92 on her first two tests and an 80 on her 3rd test. What will be her highest possible average after the 4th test?

9. If $6x + 6y = 180$, what is the mean of x and y?

10. The average (arithmetic mean) of 1, 3, 6, 12, and x is 4. The average (arithmetic mean) of 2, 4 and y is 6. What is the value of x + y?

11. The average (arithmetic mean) of a set of six numbers is 9. When a seventh number is added to the set, the average of the seven numbers is still 9. What number was added to the set?

12. The numbers 1-20 written on balls were put into a popper. One ball was chosen at random. What is the probability of drawing a ball with the number 8?

13. Emma offers her brother a random bill from her wallet. If she has 8 five-dollar bills, four ten-dollar bills and eight twenty-dollar bills in her wallet, what is the probability that her brother will receive a five-dollar bill?

Survey Results

Answer	Percent
Never	34.3%
Rarely	21.3%
Often	13.1%
Always	31.3%

14. The table above shows the results of a survey in which runners were asked how often they use protein enhancements on their long runs (ten or more miles). What is the probability of a random runner answering anything except never?

15. The 25-member National Honor Society is going to draw straws to choose their Principal's Counsel representative. The Principal's Counsel representative cannot be any of the four National Honor Society officers, what is the probability that Priya, who is not an officer, will be chosen.

16. A jar contains various colors of marbles including 7 red marbles, 9 yellow marbles and 8 green marbles. How many additional green marbles must be added to the 24 marbles already in the bag so that the probability of drawing a red marble is ⅕?

Customer Purchases at Ye Olde Sub Pub

	Soda Purchased	Soda not Purchased	Total
Sandwich Purchased	75	30	105
Sandwich not purchased	15	40	55
Total	90	70	160

17. On Saturday afternoon, the Ye Ole Sub Pub had 160 customers. The table above summarizes the purchases (the shop only sells sandwiches and sodas). What is the probability that a customer purchased a sandwich and soda OR no sandwich and no soda?

18. Willie's backyard is 5 acres (1 acre = 43,560 square feet). Willie's rocket club is making bets on what is the probability that an expended rocket will land in the swimming pool (2750 square feet)?

19. David and Julia are planning to go camping on Skyline Drive. There is a 20% chance of rain on the Saturday and Sunday that they are camping, Given that the chance of rain is independent of the day, what is the probability it will rain both days.

20. Students are playing a musical chairs game in Mrs. Ferri's class. There are seven students and six chairs. In how many configurations can the seven students fill the six chairs (one student will not be able to sit in a chair). Each chair will only accommodate one student each.

21. Governor Livingston High School needs to hire substitute teachers for their SAT Exam administration. In all, they will need 160 exam administration positions to be filled by the substitute teacher applicants. If the past shows that only 75% of applicants will show up for the interview and a third of those are not qualified for the position, how many applicants should the high school plan to invite for an interview?

22. State the relationship of the data in the scatter plots below (positive, negative or none)

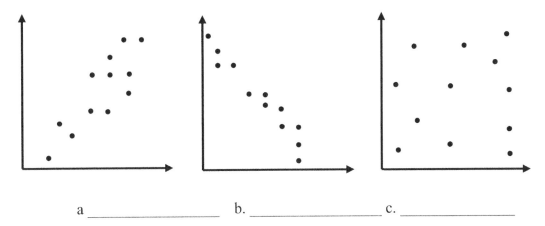

a _____ b. _____ c. _____

23. Find the range and interquartile range of the following data:

[6, 6, 6, 7, 8, 8, 8, 8, 8, 9, 10]

24. What is the probability of picking a king out of a regular 52-card deck, replacing it and then picking the same king out of the deck?

	Enrolled at Community College	Enrolled at four-year University
Male	12	8
Female	24	6

25. What is the probability that a student is enrolled at a four-year university given that he is male?

26. Classify the following probability as independent or dependent.

A customer in the post office line is selected at random and he steps out of the line. A second customer is chosen from the people remaining in the line.

27. Classify the following probability as independent or dependent.

Abby tosses a single six-sided dice. She rolls a six. What is the probability of her rolling a second six?

28. The Commonwealth of Virginia is designing license plates with three letters and three letters. All numbers and letters may be used more than once. How many different license plates can the Commonwealth create?

29. What is the likelihood of designing any given license plate if there is no requirement that each plate is unique?

30. You are making ice cream sundaes with three toppings and two flavors of ice cream. Each sundae uses one flavor of ice-cream and two scoops of toppings. How many different types of sundaes can you make?

1. The average of 6 and x is z. What is x in terms of 6 and z?

2. If 12 students earned an average grade of 88 on a test and 8 other students earned an average of 91, what would the average of the whole group be?

3. An 80-gallon baby pool is 60% full. If the water is then poured into a 60-gallon baby pool, what percent of the smaller pool is filled?

4. If a co-ed dorm houses 40% men and there are 120 women, how many men are in the dorm?

5. A fast food egg machine can make 60 eggs in nine seconds, how many eggs can it make in six minutes?

6. In cleaning out her closet, Joanne notices that the ratio of jeans to dress pants to skirts is 2 : 5 : 7. If she has a total of 140 dress pants, skirts and jeans, how many pairs of jeans does she have?

7. Find the inverse of the function $f(x) = -\frac{2}{3}x + 1$

8. Simplify i^7.

9. If David's goal is to retire with $1,450,000 at the age of 62 and he is earning interest at the annual rate of 11%, how much money must he invest at the age of:
   a) 32
   b) 42
   c) 52

10. If 9 students can clean a school in 12 hours, how long would it take 3 students?

11. If $f(x) = 2x + 1$ and $g(x) = x^2 - 3x + 4$, find:
    a) $(f * g)(x)$
    b) $(f + g)(x)$
    c) $(f - g)(x)$

12. What is the quotient of $\frac{3+2i}{4+6i}$?

13. If $f(x) = 2x + 4$ and $g(x) = -x^2 + 5$, find $f(g(x))$ and $g(f(x))$.

14. Simplify $\left(\frac{1}{1-i}\right)^2$.

15. If $f(x) = 4x^2 + 2x + 2$, find $f(2)$ and $f(-5)$.

16. A sports utility vehicle holds 35 gallons of gas and is $\frac{5}{7}$ full. How much will it cost to fill the tank at \$3.53 per gallon?

17. If $f(x) = 3x + 1$, find $f^{-1}(7)$.

18. The population of the United States in the year 1980 was 227,224,681. If the population grows at a continuous rate of 0.9%, what will the population be in 1990?

19. Let the function f be defined by $f(x) = 6x - 3a$, where a is a constant. If $f(10) + f(5) = 60$, what is the value of a?

20. If Georgia has an 82.3% in AP US History class and the last test is worth 18% of her grade, can she earn a 100% in the class?

Algebra Unit 16:
Advanced Statistics: Integrity of Samples, Variance, Standard Deviation

Define

1. Data: _____

2. Population: _____

3. Sample: _____

4. Integrity of Sample: _____

5. Variance: _____

6. Standard Deviation: _____

7. Normal Distribution: _____

8. Permutation: _____

9. Combination: _____

10. Factorial: _____

Notes:

Normal Distribution:

Using the empirical rule in a normal distribution

2.35%	13.5%	34%	34%	13.5%	2.35%	

700	850	1000	1150	1300	1450	1000
M - 3SD	M - 2SD	M - 1SD	M	M + 1SD	M + 2SD	M + 3SD

99.7%
95%
68%

Solve:

1. Is order important in a permutation?

2. Is order important in a combination?

3. Solve: $_5C_3$

4. Solve: $_9C_4$

5. Does the following sample have statistical integrity?

   Governor Livingston High School wanted to determine how many hours its average student spent on homework per evening. They decided to poll the attendees of a National Honor Society meeting.

6. The weights, in pounds, for 30 dogs at a kennel were reported. The mean, median, range, and standard deviation for the data were found. The dog with the lowest weight was 8 pounds less than its reported weight. Which of the four values above is not changed by this error?

7. Melissa is preparing candy bags for an upcoming party. She has five different flavors of candy: fruit punch, blueberry, lime, banana, and chocolate. Each candy bag will have three candies in it. If Melissa will sort the bags into piles based on which candies are in each bag, how many piles of bags could there be?

8. 20 horses are competing in a horse-racing tournament. After the final race, the names of the first, second, third, fourth, and fifth place horses will be published online. How many different possible standings are there?

9. Air traffic control needs to vector five airplanes into Dulles International Airport for landing. How many sequences of airplanes are possible?

10. An oil drilling company is prospecting in a remote area of North Dakota for drilling. In order to determine if oil is present, the oil company needs to know the types of rock in the first five rock layers. In North Dakota there are ten types of rock layers (i.e. shale, granite, lignite, etc.). How many rock compositions are possible that are relevant to the oil company?

Algebra Unit 17: Basic Trigonometry

Notes:

Both the SAT and the ACT Exams will expect test-takers to have a basic understanding of trigonometry. This includes the two special trigonometric triangles (30-60-90) and (45-45-90) and the trigonometric unit circle. In this unit, we will introduce the two special triangles.

1. The foundation of trigonometry is triangles and the relationship of sides and angles.

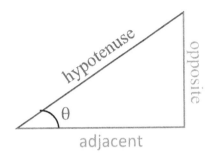

2. The two fundamental triangles ALWAYS follow specific ratios.

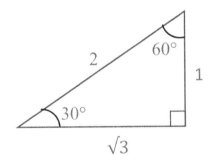

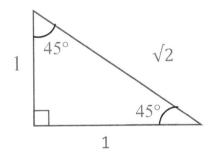

3. Sine, cosine and tangent are ratios of the triangles' legs divided by each other or by the hypotenuse. Students remember the ratios by the mnemonic: SOH–CAH–TOA. The mnemonic stands for:

Sine θ = opposite (leg) / hypotenuse

Cosine θ = adjacent (leg) / hypotenuse

Tangent θ = opposite (leg) / adjacent (leg)

4. If you have not been exposed to trigonometry in school yet, try to memorize the chart below:

θ	0°	30°	45°	60°	90°
$\sin \theta$	0	$\dfrac{1}{2}$	$\dfrac{\sqrt{2}}{2}$	$\dfrac{\sqrt{3}}{2}$	1
$\cos \theta$	1	$\dfrac{\sqrt{3}}{2}$	$\dfrac{\sqrt{2}}{2}$	$\dfrac{1}{2}$	0
$\tan \theta$	0	$\dfrac{\sqrt{3}}{3}$	1	$\sqrt{3}$	undef.

5. You may also want to refer to the trigonometric unit circle below:

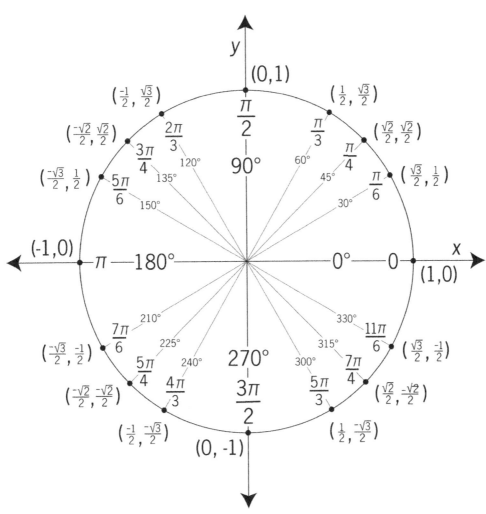

6. Define:

Radian: _____

Degrees: _____

7. Converting radians to degrees and degrees to radians:

- Degrees to radians: Multiply degrees by π/180. For example:
  60° * π/180 = π/3 radians

- Radians to degrees: Multiply radians by 180/π. For example:
  π/4 * 180/4 = 45°

Solve:

Evaluate the trigonometric functions for the triangle below.

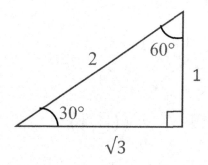

1. Sin 30° =

2. Cos 30° =

3. Tan 30° =

4. Sin 60° =

5. Cos 60° =

6.   Tan 60° =

Evaluate the trigonometric functions for the triangle below.

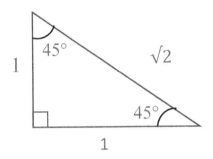

7.   Sin 45° =

8.   Cos 45° =

9.   Tan 45° =

Evaluate the trigonometric functions for the triangle below.

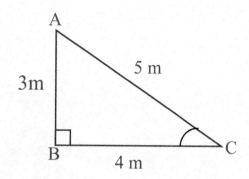

10. Sin A =

11. Cos A =

12. Tan A =

13. Sin C =

14. Cos C =

15. Tan C =

Draw a triangle for each of the following problems and find the sine, cosine and tangent for each question:

16. Sin θ = $\frac{1}{2}$ Cos: Tan:

17. Sin θ = 1/3   Cos: Tan:

18. Tan θ = 1/5   Cos: Sin:

19. If triangles ABC and DEF are similar and the cosine of angle B is 5/13, what is the cosine of angle E?

20. If sin x = a, what is the cosine of angle x?

21. Triangle ABC has a right angle at A. If the sin C = ⅘, what is the value of the tan A?

22. If the sin of angle A = 7/9, what is the cosine of angle A?

23. If a line through the origin and (5,6) forms a triangle with the X-axis with angle measure θ, what are its six trigonometric measures?

    a) Sin:

    b) Cosine:

    c) Tangent:

    d) Cosecant:

    e) Secant:

    f) Cotangent:

24. In a triangle ABC, the measure of $\angle B$ is 90°, BC = 12, and AC = 13. Triangle DEF is similar to triangle ABC, where vertices D, E, and F correspond to vertices A, B, and C, respectively, and each side of triangle DEF is $\frac{1}{4}$ the length of the corresponding side of triangle ABC. What is the value of sin (F) ?

25. In right triangle JKL, the measure of ∠L is 90°, hypotenuse JK = 5 units, and side KL = 2 units. What is tan (K) ?

26. In a right triangle, one angle measures x°, where $\cos x° = \frac{3}{5}$. What is $\sin (90° - x°)$?

27. The area of a right triangle is 50. One of its angles is 45°. Find the lengths of the sides and hypotenuse of the triangle.

28. Julia props up a ladder against a wall. The ladder makes an angle of 25° from the ground. If the ladder is 12 feet long, which of the following is the expression for finding the distance the foot of the ladder is from the wall?

    a) 12 cos 25°

    b) $\sin \frac{10}{25}$

    c) $\cos \frac{10}{25}$

    d) 12 sin 25°

    e) 12 tan 25°

29. In right triangle ABC, if $sin\ A = 0.5$ and side $BC = 10$, find the length of the hypotenuse, AB, and side AC.

30. Name three pythagorean triples.

Algebra Unit 18: Advanced Trigonometry

Notes:

1. Generally, the SAT Exam will not require knowledge of advanced trigonometry including the trigonometric unit circle and the pythagorean identities. On the other hand, The ACT Exam will have several questions which expect a knowledge of standard sine and cosine graphs, inverses and identities such as pythagorean identities and cofunction identities.

2. Pythagorean Identities:

   a) $\sin^2\theta, + \cos^2\theta = 1$

   b) $\tan^2\theta, - \sec^2\theta = 1$

   c) $\cot^2\theta - \csc^2\theta = 1$

3. Cofunction Identities:

   a) $\sin(\pi/2 - \theta) = \cos\theta$

   b) $\cos(\pi/2 - \theta) = \sin\theta$

   c) $\tan(\pi/2 - \theta) = \cot\theta$

   d) $\cot(\pi/2 - \theta) = \tan\theta$

   e) $\csc(\pi/2 - \theta) = \sec\theta$

   f) $\sec(\pi/2 - \theta) = \csc\theta$

4. Sum and Difference Identities:

   a. $\sin(x + y) = \sin x \cos y + \cos x \sin y$

   b. $\sin(x - y) = \sin x \cos y - \cos x \sin y$

   c. $\cos(x + y) = \cos x \cos y - \sin x \sin y$

   d. $\cos(x - y) = \cos x \cos y + \sin x \sin y$

5. Signs of quadrants: Memorize the mnemonic: All Students Take Calculus (ASTC)

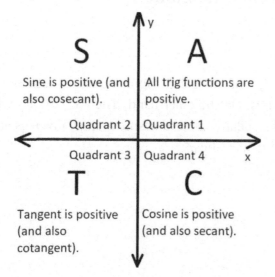

a. All six trig functions are positive in Quadrant I.

b. Only the SINE and COSECANT are positive in Quadrant II.

c. Only the TANGENT AND COTANGENT are positive in Quadrant III.

d. Only the COSINE and SECANT are positive in Quadrant IV.

6. Standard forms of trigonometric curves: The exams will not likely not expect students to answer questions on any trig curves beyond the sine and cosine graphs.

a. Sine graph: y = a sin b (x +/- h) +/- k

b. Cosine graph: y = a cos b (x +/- h) +/- k

c. a = amplitude (height of the curve)

d. b is used to calculate the period of the graph (one complete cycle of the function)

e. h is the horizontal translation of the equation. The graph translates left with a + and right with a -.

f. k is the vertical translation of the equation. The graph translates up with a + sign and down with a - sign.

Practice Problems

Graph the following equations:

1. y = sin x

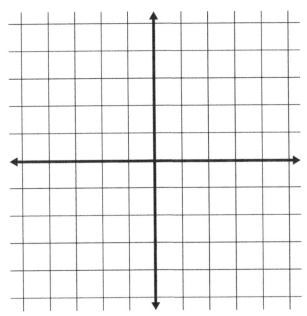

2. $y = \cos x$

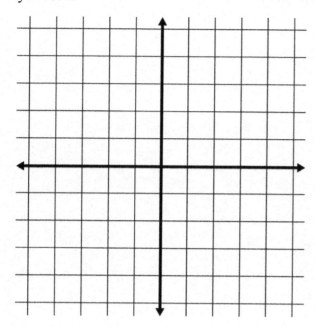

3. y = 3 cos x

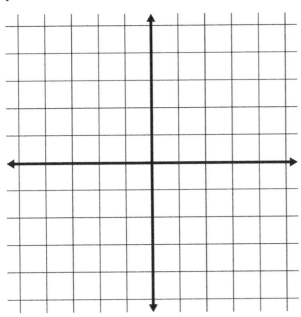

4. y = 3 sin x

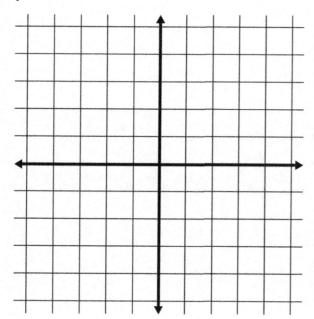

5. $y = 2 \cos 2 (x - 2) + 2$

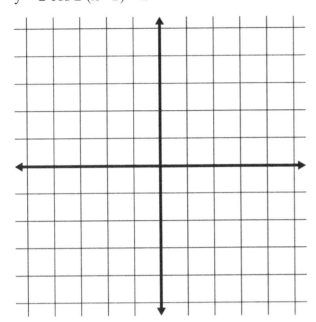

6. $y = 2 \sin 2 (x - 2) + 2$

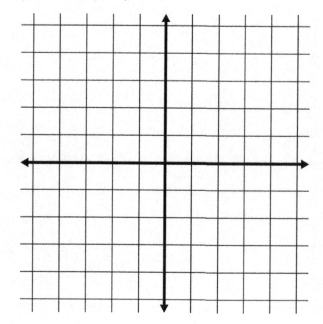

Given the function $f(x) = 4 \sin 8 (x - 3) + 6$

7. What is the amplitude?

8. What is the period?

9. What is the phase (horizontal shift)?

10. What is the vertical shift?

11. What is the domain?

12. What is the range?

13. What trig identity does the following function represent?:

    sin (60) (cos 30) + (cos 60) (sin 30)

14. Solve $(\sin^2 30 + \cos^2 30) = ?$

15. Graph $f(x) = \sin x$ over the domain of $-\pi/2 < x < \pi/2$

Chapter 8

Geometry

In this chapter:
• Geometry Concepts: Angles, Triangles, Polygons and Circles • Four Units of Exercises

1. Angles

2. Triangles

3. Quadrilaterals

4. Circles

Geometry Unit 1: Angles

Definitions & Properties:

Angle: An angle is made up of two rays that have the same initial point. The initial (meeting) point of the rays is the vertex of the angle. An angle may be named by is vertex (single point) or by its three points, e.g.:

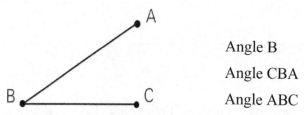

Angle B

Angle CBA

Angle ABC

Classifying Angles: Angles are classified by their degree measure:

Acute Angle:	Angle of $< 90°$
Right Angle:	Angle of $90°$
Obtuse Angle:	Angle of $> 90°$ but $< 180°$
Straight Angle:	Angle of exactly $180°$
Complementary Angles:	Two angles that add to $90°$
Supplementary Angles:	Two angles that add to $180°$
Linear Pair:	Two angles that form a straight angle, adding to $180°$
Congruent Angles:	Angles with equal degree measure

Special Formations of Angles:

Angle Bisector: A line or line segment that divides an angle exactly in half at the angle's vertex, creating two equal angles.

Perpendicular Lines: Perpendicular lines and line segments from right angles (90°), denoted by:

Parallel Lines: Two or more lines in the same plane that never meet, have equal slopes, and remain equidistant from each other for infinity. When parallel lines are cut by a transversal, they form a series of specially defined angles.

Transversal: A line that cuts 2 or more parallel lines.

Congruent Angles Formed by Parallel Lines Cut by a Transversal:

If two or more parallel lines are intersected by a transversal, special angle relationships are formed.

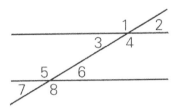

Corresponding Angles:

Angles that are in similar positions are equal:

Angles 1 & 5

Angles 2 & 6

Angles 3 & 7

Angles 4 & 8

Alternate Interior Angles:

Angles that are in similar positions inside the parallel lines, are opposite of each other and have equal degree measure:

Angles 3 & 6

Angles 4 & 5

Same Side Interior Angles:

Same side interior angles are supplementary (= 180°):

Angles 4 & 6

Angles 3 & 5

Alternate Exterior Angles:

Angles that are in similar positions outside the parallel lines, are opposite of each other and have equal degree measure:

Angles 1 & 8

Angles 2 & 7

Same Side Exterior Angles:

Same side exterior angles are supplementary (= 180°):

Angles 1 & 7

Angles 2 & 8

Vertical Angles:

Angles that form an "X" and are opposite each other:

Angles 1 & 4

Angles 2 & 3

Angles 5 & 8

Angles 6 & 7

***<u>NOTE</u>: The angles delineated above are only equal if the two (or more lines) cut by the transversal are <u>parallel</u>. The SAT problem <u>must</u> specify that the lines are parallel!!!

Practice Problems

1. Given: Line A is parallel to line B and Lines A and B are cut by the transversal, line C and $\angle2 = 42°$

   What are the measures of these angles?

   a. $\angle1 =$

   b. $\angle2 = 42°$

   c. $\angle3 =$

   d. $\angle4 =$

   e. $\angle5 =$

   f. $\angle6 =$

   g. $\angle7 =$

   h. $\angle8 =$

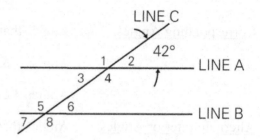

Figure not drawn to scale

2. If $\angle1 = Y°$, in terms of Y, what is the measure of each angle?

   a. $\angle1 = Y°$

   b. $\angle2 =$

   c. $\angle3 =$

   d. $\angle4 =$

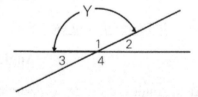

Figure not drawn to scale

3. Given: Line P is parallel to Line N and Lines P and N are cut by the transversal, Line M

$\angle 6 = 2X + 10°$ and $\angle 8 = 5X - 40°$

What are the measures of the following angles?

a. $\angle 1 =$

b. $\angle 2 =$

c. $\angle 3 =$

d. $\angle 4 =$

e. $\angle 5 =$

f. $\angle 6 =$

g. $\angle 7 =$

h. $\angle 8 =$

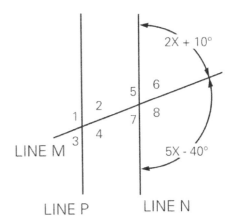

Figure not drawn to scale

4. Given: $\angle A = 140°$ and $\angle E = 155°$

What are the measures of the following angles?

a. $\angle A = 140°$

b. $\angle B =$

c. $\angle C =$

d. $\angle D =$

e. $\angle E = 155°$

f. $\angle F =$

g. $\angle G =$

h. $\angle H =$

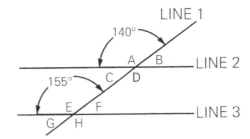

Figure not drawn to scale

5. What is the measure of angle AOB?

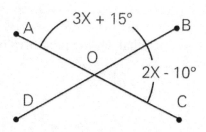

Figure not drawn to scale

6. Given: Line N is parallel to Line P

   What is the measure of ∠ABC?

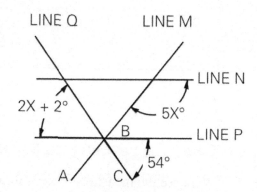

Figure not drawn to scale

7. Two angles are complementary. If one angle equals 31°, what is the measure of the sum of the angles?

8. Two angles are supplementary. If one angle equals 31°, what is the measure of the other angle?

9. Ray OL bisects ∠MON. The measure of ∠MOL is 11x° and the measure of ∠LON is (4x +19)°. What is the measure of ∠MON?

10. If a right angle is made up of three smaller angles such that:

$\angle A = x$ $\qquad$ $\angle B = 2x$ $\qquad$ $\angle C = 3x$

What is the measure of the largest angle?

Geometry Unit 2: Triangles

Definitions:

Triangle: A 3-sided closed figure, named by its vertices (points where two sides meet). e.g.: Δ ABC

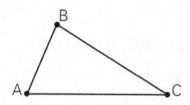

Vertex: The common endpoint of two sides of a triangle.

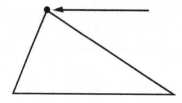

Leg: A side of a triangle (non-hypotenuse and non-base).

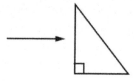

Base: In an isosceles triangle, the third non-congruent side of a triangle.

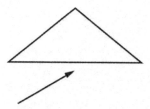

Hypotenuse: In a right triangle, the side opposite the right angle.

Altitude: A perpendicular segment connecting the vertex and its non-included side.

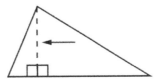

Median: A segment whose endpoints are the vertex of a triangle and the midpoint of the opposite
side.

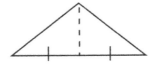

Perimeter: The sum of the lengths of the three sides of a triangle.

Area: The number of square units needed to cover a surface.

Area of a $\Delta = \frac{1}{2}$ base $*$ height

Note: Some triangles need an altitude to compute area.

Properties:

1. The sum of the angles in a triangle is always $180°$.

2. There can be at most one right or one obtuse angle in a triangle.

3. Size of the angle controls the length of the sides. Longer sides are across from larger angles and smaller sides are across from smaller angles.

4. The sum of the lengths of two sides of a triangle may not equal more than the measure of the third side.

5. Exterior angles are formed by extending one of the sides.

6. The exterior angle is equal to the sum of the two remote nterior angles in the triangle.

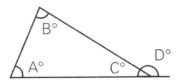

The exterior angle (D) is equal to the sum of the two remote interior angles (A + B).

Pythagorean Theorem

In a right triangle, the sum of the squares of the measures of the legs equals the square of the measure of the hypotenuse: $a^2 + b^2 = c^2$

Pythagorean Triples:

$3 - 4 - 5$

$5 - 12 - 13$

$8 - 15 - 17$

$7 - 24 - 25$

** These triples may be multiplied by any common factor and remain Pythagorean triples.

Classifying Triangles

Triangles may be classified by their sides and/or their angles.

<u>By Sides:</u>   Scalene $\triangle$: Has no congruent sides

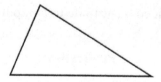

<u>Isosceles $\triangle$</u>: Has two congruent sides, called legs

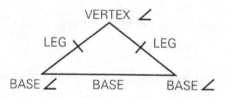

<u>Equilateral $\triangle$</u>: Has three congruent sides and three congruent angles

By Angles:

Acute Δ: Has three angles with measures of < *90°*

Right Δ: Has one angle of 90°, formed by two perpendicular sides.

Obtuse Δ: Has one angle with measure of >90°

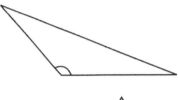

Equiangular Δ: Has three equal angles and three equal sides.

Similar Triangles: All six parts of one triangle will be in the same ratio to all six parts of another triangle.

Congruent Triangles: All six parts (three angles and three sides) of one triangle must be congruent to all six parts of another triangle.

Methods of Proving Congruency:

Side-Side-Side (SSS): The three sides of one triangle must be congruent to the three sides of another triangle.

Side-Angle-Side (SAS):   Two sides and the angle between the two sides must be congruent to the two sides and their included angle of another triangle.

<u>Angle-Side-Angle (ASA)</u>:   Two angles and the included side of one triangle must be congruent to two angles and the included side of the other triangle.

<u>Angle-Angle-Side (AAS)</u>:   Two angles and a non-included side of one triangle must be congruent to the corresponding two angles and side of the other triangle.

<u>Angle-Side-Side (ASS)</u>:   This proof never works – ever!!!! Do not be fooled!!!

<u>2 Angles</u>:   If two angles of a triangle are congruent then the third angle of the triangles is congruent. Thus, the two triangles are similar, but not necessarily congruent.

Special Ratios of Congruency:

<u>Perimeter</u>:   The perimeter of two congruent triangles will have the same ratio as the two perimeters.

<u>Area</u>:   The ratio of the areas of two congruent triangles is the square of the ratio of the sides.

Special Right Triangles:

Special right triangles form the basis of trigonometry. The two special right triangles used in the SAT will be the 30° − 60° − 90° triangle and the 45° − 45° − 90° triangle. These two right triangles will always preserve the same angle/side ratios.

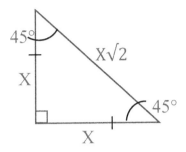

Practice Problems

Find the missing variable(s). Classify the triangles by their angles and their sides. Note: The figures are not drawn to scale.

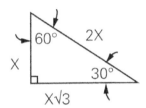

1.

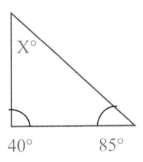

2.

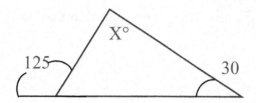

3.

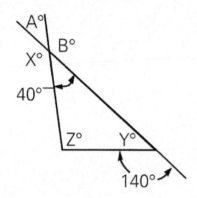

a. A=

b. B=

c. X=

d. Y=

e. Z=

4.

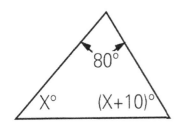

80°

X°   (X+10)°

    a. X =

    b. X + 10 =

5. Given ∠J = ∠K

    a. A =

    b. B =

    c. C =

    d. D =

    e. E =

    f. F =

    g. G =

    h. H =

    i. I =

    j. J =

    k. K =

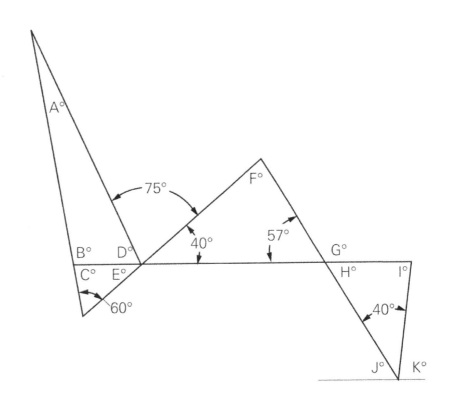

6. If the right triangle below, solve for X =

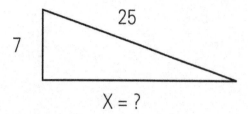

$X = ?$

Classify the following triangles by their sides and angles and determine congruency

7.

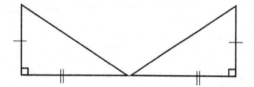

    a. Sides:

    b. Congruency:

8.

9. Given ΔXYZ ≈ ΔABC

    ∠Y = 57°

    ∠A = 64°

    ∠Z = (5t + 4)°

    Solve for t.

10. What is value of ∠ ABC?

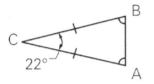

11. Given equilateral ΔFGH with side FG = 8, what is the area of the triangle?

12. Find the area of ΔBCD.

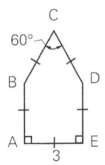

13. Area of Δ FGH = 12 inches^2 and the height is 6 inches

Solve for x

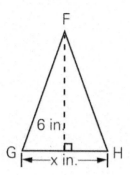

14. Find the area of an equiangular triangle whose perimeter is 48 inches.

15. Solve for Y/2 if the area of the following triangle is 48 square inches.

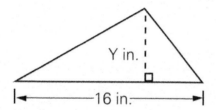

16. Find the value of all 3 angles and the remaining two sides.

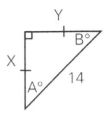

17. If the perimeter of the triangle below is $6 + 3\sqrt{2}$, what is the value of:

X =

Y =

A =

B =

Area of the triangle =

18. Given EBCD is a square, what is the area of the entire polygon?

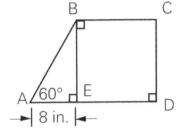

19. Given two equilateral triangles, A and B, what is the ratio of the sides of $\triangle A$ to $\triangle B$?

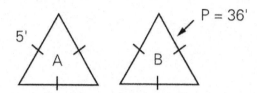

5'

A

B

P = 36'

Figures not drawn to scale

20. What is the value of $X^2 + Y^2$?

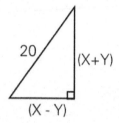

20

(X+Y)

(X - Y)

Geometry Unit 3: Polygons with 360° or more

Definitions & Properties:

Polygon: A closed (concave, non-convex) figure with three or more sides, formed with a finite number of coplanar segments. Polygons are classified by the relationship of their sides and angles.

Regular Polygon: Also called a convex polygon, all sides and angles are congruent.

Quadrilateral: A polygon which has four sides and four angles.

Parallelogram: A quadrilateral with the following characteristics:

1) Two pairs of parallel sides

2) Opposite sides are congruent

3) Diagonals bisect each other

4) Same side angles are supplementary

Rectangle: A parallelogram with the following characteristics:

- Four right (90°) angles

- Congruent diagonals

Rhombus: A parallelogram with the following characteristics:

- All sides congruent

- Diagonals are perpendicular

- Diagonals bisect each other

- Diagonals bisect opposite angles

Trapezoid: A quadrilateral with exactly one pair of parallel sides called bases. If the legs are congruent, the trapezoid is called isosceles.

Square: A parallelogram with all sides congruent and all angles congruent (right and 90°).

Pentagon: A polygon with five sides

Hexagon: A polygon with six sides

Heptagon: A polygon with seven sides

Octagon: A polygon with eight sides

Nonagon: A polygon with nine sides

Decagon: A polygon with ten sides

Sides/Angles: Any regular polygon has the same number of sides and angles, e.g., a square has 4 sides and 4 angles

No. of Triangles: To compute the number of triangles in any polygon:

Number of sides − 2

Total Degrees: To compute the total degrees in any polygon:

(Number of sides − 2) ∗ 180 or $(n - 2) * 180$

Angle Measure: To compute the measure of each individual angle in a polygon, begin with the equation above and secondly divide the result by the number of sides/angles in the polygon.

$$\frac{(n-2)*180}{n}$$

Formulas

Area of most quadrilaterals: base ∗ height = units^2

Area of trapezoids: $\frac{1}{2}$ height (base$_1$ + base$_2$) = units^2

Volume of most polygons: area of base ∗ height = units^3

Practice Problems

1. Find the total angle measure of each figure:

   a. Triangle

   b. Quadrilateral

   c. Rhombus

   d. Pentagon

   e. Hexagon

   f. Heptagon

g. Octagon

h. Nonagon

i. Decagon

2. What is the measure of the fourth angle in a quadrilateral if the others are 40°, 100°, and 70°?

3. Find the measure of the smallest angle of a quadrilateral if the total interior angle measure equals $x + 5, x + 8, x + 20,$ and $x + 35$.

4. One angle of a parallelogram = 38°, find the other three angles.

5. Find the diagonals, perimeter and area of a square with sides of 24 feet.

6. How many triangles are in an octagon?

7. Find the area of figure DEFG.

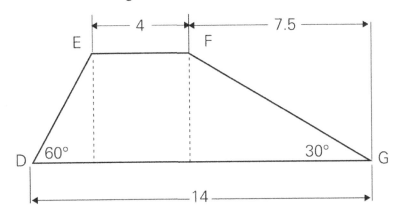

8. If ABCDEF is a regular hexagon, what is the value of ∠FAB?

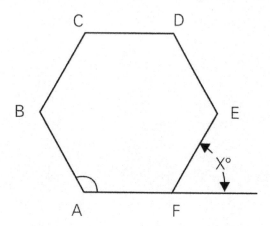

9. What is the value of ∠X in the hexagon in problem number 8?

10. Find the area and perimeter of the isosceles trapezoid below.

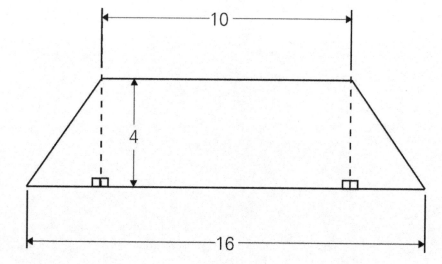

11. The area of an isosceles trapezoid is 36 cm². Its perimeter is 28 cm and one leg is 5 cm, what is its height?

12. ABCD is a square with diagonals intersecting at E. AB = 3. What is:

    a. AC

    b. DE

13. MNOP is a rectangle, QMRN is a rhombus. Find:

    a. ∠ NQM

    b. ∠ MRO

    c. ∠ ORP

    d. ∠ NPO

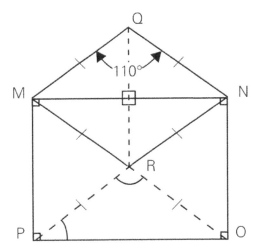

14. Given ABCD is a square, find the length of BC given that:

    a. AB = *1 + 10x*

    b. CD = *13 + 3x*

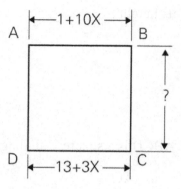

15. What is the volume of a rectangular prism with length of 5, height of 10 and width of 2?

Geometry Unit 4: Circles

Definitions & Properties:

Circle:

A set of points that consists of all points in a plane that are equidistant from the center of a circle.

Naming:

A circle is named by its center.

Circle A:

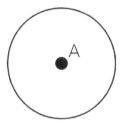

Radius:

Line segment with one endpoint at the center of a circle and one endpoint on the circle itself.

Radius AB:

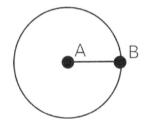

Chord:

A line segment whose endpoints are on the circle, but not necessarily through the center.

Chord CD:

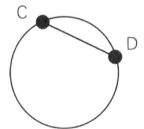

Diameter:	A chord that goes through the center of the circle, the longest possible chord in a circle.

Diameter EF:

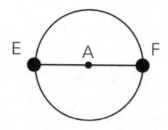

Degree Measure:	360°

Central Angle: An angle whose vertex is at the center of the circle. May measure between 0° and 360°.

Central Angle GAH:

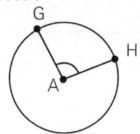

Arcs:	An unbroken part of a circle, created by a central angle. Arc GH is created by the central angle GAH.

Arc GH:

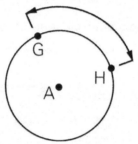

Minor Arc:	An arc with a measure of less than 180°.

Minor Arc IK:

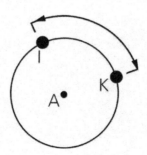

Major Arc:	An arc with a measure of more than 180°.

Major Arc LMN:

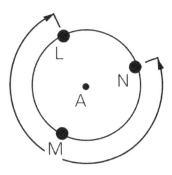

Semicircle:	The arc (½ circle) is created by a 180° central angle.

Semicircle OAP:

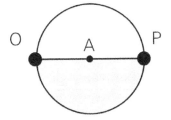

Sector:	A pie-shaped piece of a circle formed by a central angle and an arc.

Sector RAS:

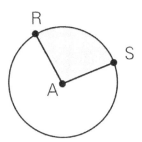

Circumference:	Linear distance around a circle. The units are always linear (not squared or cubed).

$C = 2 * \pi * \text{radius}$ or $\pi * \text{diameter}$
$2\pi r$ or πD

<u>Area of a Circle</u>:   The number of square units within a circle.

$$A = \pi * \text{radius}^2 \quad \text{or} \quad A = \pi \left(\tfrac{1}{2}D\right)^2$$

<u>Arc Length</u>:   Linear distance of the arc. The length of the arc is the part of the circumference proportional to the measure of the central angle to 360°.

$$\frac{\text{Arc length}}{\text{Circumference}} = \frac{\text{Central angle}}{360°}$$

<u>Area of a sector</u>:   Number of square units within a sector of a circle. The area of the sector is proportional to the area of the circle.

$$\frac{\text{Sector area}}{\text{Area of circle}} = \frac{\text{Central angle}}{360°}$$

<u>Concentric Circle</u>:   Two or more circles, one within the other(s), sharing the same center.

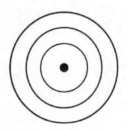

<u>Pi</u>:   Represented by the symbol π. Its value is approximately 22/7 or 3.14159…

<u>Volume of a cylinder</u>: π * radius^2 * height

$$\pi r^2 h$$

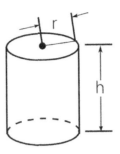

1. Given Circle A:

   a. Name all chords.

   b. Name two diameters.

   c. Name four radii.

   d. Name a chord that is not a diameter.

   e. If DA = 5, what is EB?

   f. Find the circumference of Circle A if EB = 8.

   g. Find the area of Circle A if DF = 12.

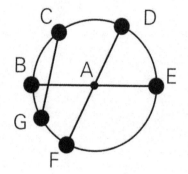

2. Given Circle B, find:

   a. Circumference of the circle.

   b. Area of the circle.

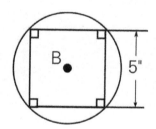

3. Given Circle C, find:

   a. Area of the circle.

   b. Area of the shaded region.

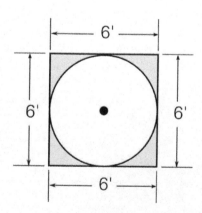

4. Given Circle E, find:

   a. Area of the circle

   b. Area of the triangle.

   c. Perimeter of the triangle

   d. Area of the circle, not included in the triangle.

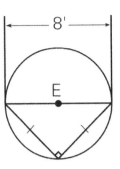

5. If AC = 6 cm in Circle A (above), find the measures of the following arcs:

   a. CD

   b. DE

   c. FB

   d. BE

   e. FC

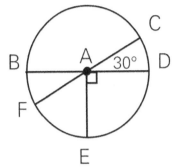

6. If AC = 7 cm in Circle A (above), find the area of the following sectors:

   a. CAD

   b. DAF

   c. FAB

7. Given Circle F, find the measures of the smallest and largest angles.

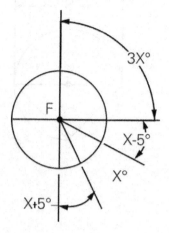

8. If the radius of a circle is tripled, what happens to the circumference and the area?

   a. Circumference:

   b. Area

9. If the area of a circle is 36π inches^2, what is the area of a sector created by a central angle of $60°$?

10. Find the thickness of a tire whose outer radius is 8 inches and whose inner radius is $5\frac{3}{8}$ inches.

11. If a horse is tethered to a fence post at an angle of 90°, and his lead line is 15 feet long, over how many square feet can he graze?

12. If a soda can has a radius of 1.5 inches and a height of 6 inches, what is its volume?

13. If a circular baby pool is 4 feet across and 12 inches high, what is its volume?

14. If a tire of diameter of 30 inches travels two miles (mile = 5280 feet),

    a) How many linear feet does it cover?

    b) How many revolutions does the tire make in its travel?

15. If the circumference of Circle H is three times the circumference of Circle I and the length of HI is 18 inches, what is the diameter of Circle I?

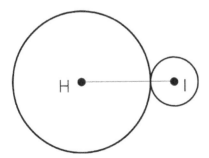

ACT Science Test

Introduction

Years ago, when I first laid eyes on the ACT Science section, I was completely, 100% intimidated. The questions looked so very difficult. My instinct was to close the big red *Official ACT Prep Guide,* and just focus on the SAT Exam. At that time, our practice, Professional Tutoring, was only teaching the SAT Exam, so I was okay with ignoring the ACT Exam. It was actually a student who encouraged me to tackle the ACT Science section. We did that together in a tutoring session. Within just a short period, I realized that the ACT Science section was fairly straightforward; it is essentially a series of case studies made up of experiments, data and data analysis. I realized that no science background was necessary to answer the questions.

Later in this chapter, we will go over the types of science passages and the best way to approach both the information and the questions. Several years ago, as we were teaching class and the students were bemoaning both the difficulty and the seeming strangeness of the questions, one student exclaimed, "This is just a really hard reading section!" And, that it is: another, more complicated reading section.

So, let's go back to the basics. The ACT science section is the fourth of the four multiple choice sections of the ACT Exam. It includes 40 questions with a 35-minute time limit and does not allow the use of a calculator. The purpose of the science section is to assess students' ability to evaluate science practices. Each passage is made up of actual scientific cases, each followed by four multiple-choice questions. The section will include six science passages, focusing on the natural sciences:

- Biology

- Chemistry

- Earth/Space Sciences (geology, astronomy, meteorology)

- Physics

  The ACT science section presents information in a variety of formats:

- Narratives

- Graphs

- Tables

- Charts

- Diagrams

A reasonable high school science background will make the information represented in the passages more familiar. The ACT Exam does not require students to have ANY science knowledge or to remember specific science facts. Rather, the exam requires the following skills:

- Reading

- Interpretation

- Analysis

- Reasoning

- Evaluation

- Problem-solving skills

The Three Types of Science Passage Formats

The Science section requires students to critically examine the information provided and the scientists' hypotheses, scientific method and the relationship between the information provided and the conclusions provided in the narratives. From there, students will often have to draw conclusions and make their own predictions.

The questions require you to recognize and understand the basic features of, and concepts related to, the provided information; to examine critically the relationship between the information provided and the conclusions drawn or hypotheses developed; and to generalize from given information to gain new information, draw conclusions, or make predictions.

Each science passage will appear in one of three formats:

- **Research Summaries** (three passages, 18 questions): This format provides information including the scientific method behind and the results of one or more related experiments. The questions focus on the organization and implementation of the experiments. The ACT is looking for students to identify the purpose, method and results for each experiment. *In Research Summary passages, students will want to focus on purpose, method and results for each experiment. Students must be able to identify, compare and contrast the differences and similarities between experiments.*

- **Data Representation** (two passages, 17 questions): This format focuses on graphs, charts and tables as found in scientific journals and texts. Students will evaluate and interpret the information provided. The ACT is looking for students to relate the data presented, and interpolate, extrapolate and understand the differences in data representation in tables and graphs. *For this type, students will want to focus on identifying variables, units and trends.*

- **Conflicting Viewpoints** (one passage, 7 questions): This format provides two or more explanations for the same scientific topics. Generally, Conflicting Viewpoints passages do not provide diagrams or any types of tables, charts, etc. The viewpoints have inherent flaws including incomplete data or differing premises. This type of format will focus on the students' ability to understand and compare different, inconsistent viewpoints, reasoning and hypotheses. *For this type, students will want to annotate the different scientific evaluations and explanations, highlighting the similarities and differences.*

The Three ACT Science Test Subscores

The ACT will report four scores for the ACT Science section:

1. An overall total score of 1-36 points

2. Interpretation of Data (~45% of total score)

3. Scientific Investigation (~25% of total score)

4. Evaluation of Models, Inferences and Experimental Results (~30%)

   1. **Interpretation of Data** questions require competent analysis of scientific data presented in graphs, tables, diagrams. Students are expected to translate data from graphs to tables and vice versa; recognize, identify and evaluate data trends; and reason mathematically.

   2. **Scientific Investigation** requires students to understand the scientific method and experiment design. Scientific investigation requires a strong ability to evaluate experimental procedures and predict the possible outcomes of additional trials.

   3. **Evaluation of Models, Inferences, and Experimental Results** requires students to judge the soundness of scientific data and form their own conclusions and predictions based on the provided information.

We promise the ACT Science section is neither as complicated nor aspotentially difficult as you might be thinking at this point. I will concede that the ACT Science section is both more complicated and more abstruse (obscure) than the other ACT sections but it is no more difficult. With practice, many students find the Science section to be the easiest of all four multiple choice sections.

Science Terms to Learn

Like the SAT Exam, the ACT Exam can be cracked with preparation. You should not go into either of these exams blind, without preparation. We are here to help you prepare with the following test preparation tips:

1. **Increase your science knowledge and fluency by memorizing and understanding the following scientific terms:**

   1. **Absolute:** existing independent of any other cause

   2. **Acceleration**: the rate of change in velocity

   3. **Accuracy:** freedom from mistake, exact

   4. **Adverse:** acting against or in an opposite direction

   5. **Allele**: a gene variant

   6. **Analogue:** similar or comparable in certain respects

   7. **Analyze:** to study the relationship of the parts of something by analysis

   8. **Application:** ability to put to a practical use, having something to do with the matter at hand

   9. **Approximately:** nearly, an estimate or figure that is almost exact

   10. **Argument:** reasoning for or against something

   11. **Assumption:** something that is accepted as true

   12. **Atom**: a particle that contains protons, neutrons and electrons;   smallest particle that can be involved in a chemical reaction

   13. **Boiling point**: temperature when liquid turns to gas

   14. **Buoyancy**: the ability to float

   15. **Cell**: the smallest independent part of an organism.

   16. **Charge**: Charge comes in two varieties: positive and negative: positive charge (+q) is a property of protons; negative charge (-q) is a property of electrons. The charge on the proton is identical in size to that on the electron, but differs in sign.

17. **Chemical Reaction**: the rearrangement of atoms to form a new substance

18. **Chromosome**: the structure of nucleic acids and proteins that carries the genetic material in a cell

19. **Concentration:** the ratio of the amount of solute to the amount of solvent or solution

20. **Conclusion:** a final decision based on facts, experience or reasoning

21. **Conduct**: heat transfer as a result of molecular interaction

22. **Confirm:** to make sure of the truth of something

23. **Consequence:** something produced by a cause of condition

24. **Consistent:** in agreement, firm, changeless

25. **Constant:** remaining steady and unchanged

26. **Contradiction:** a statement in opposition to another

27. **Control Group:** experimental group in which conditions are controlled

28. **Controlled Experiment:** one in which the condition suspected to cause and effect is compared to one without the suspected condition

29. **Controlled Variable:** a factor in an experiment that remains constant

30. **Convection**: heat transfer from fluid movement.

31. **Correlation:** a close connection between two ideas or two sets of data

32. **Criticism**: a finding of fault; disapproval

33. **Definitive:** most nearly complete or accurate

34. **Demonstrate:** to explain by use of examples or experiments

35. **Density**: the mass per volume of a substance.

36. **Dependence:** a state of being controlled by something else

37. **Dependent Variable:** result or change that occurs due to the part of an experiment being tested

38. **Diminish**: to make smaller or less; to decrease in size

39. **Direct Relationship:** the connection between two variables that shows the same effect (they both increase or both decrease)

40. **Effective:** producing or able to produce a desired condition

41. **Elasticity**: the ability of a substance to return to its original shape

42. **Electrons**: Negatively charged atomic particles

43. **Elements**: a substance/atom that cannot be split into smaller components

44. **Estimation:** forming a calculation based on incomplete data

45. **Ethical:** following accepted rules and behavior

46. **Evaluation:** the result of finding something; estimating the value of something

47. **Evidence:** that which serves to prove or disprove something

48. **Examine:** to look at or check carefully

49. **Expectation:** the extent of a chance that something will occur

50. **Experiment:** a test made to find something out

51. **Experimental Design:** the plan for a controlled experiment

52. **Experimental Group:** the experimental part in which all conditions are kept the same except for the condition being tested

53. **Explanation:** a statement that makes something clear

54. **Extrapolation:** estimating a value of another characteristic beyond the range of a given value of another characteristic

55. **Figure:** a picture that explains

56. **Fluid**: liquid or gas

57. **Fundamental:** a basic part

58. **Gamete**: a sex cell that carries both parents' genes

59. **Gene**: a section of DNA that determines inheritance

60. **Generalization:** something given as a broad statement or conclusion

61. **Gravity**: force that attracts an object to the center of the earth.

62. **Hypothesis:** testable explanation of a question or problem

63. **Illustrate:** to make clear by using examples

64. **Imply:** to suggest rather than to say plainly

65. **Inconsistent:** not in agreement

66. **Incorporate:** to join or unite closely in a single body

67. **Independent Variable:** in a controlled experiment, the variable that is being changed

68. **Indication:** the act of pointing out or pointing to something

69. **Indicator:** any device that measures, records, or visibly points out something

70. **Inertia**: the tendency of a body at rest to stay at rest

71. **Indirect Relationship**: As the independent variable increases or decreases, the dependent variable does the opposite

72. **Ingredient:** any of the components of which something is made

73. **Interpolation:** estimating a value that falls between two known values

74. **Interpretation:** the act of telling the meaning of something; explanation

75. **Inverse Relationship (indirect):** the connection between two variables that shows the opposite effect (e.g., when the value of one increases, the value of the other decreases)

76. **Investigate:** to study by close and careful observation

77. **Ion**: Atom with an unbalanced electrical charge due to loss/gain of electrons

78. **Irregular:** not continuous or coming at settimes

79. **Issue:** something that is in question

80. **Judgment:** an opinion formed by examining and comparing

81. **Justify:** to prove or show to be right or reasonable

82. **Kinetic Energy:** the energy of a body in motion

83. **Legend:** a title, description, or key accompanying a figure or map

84. **Mass**: the quantity of matter in a body

85. **Maximum:** as great as possible in amount or degree

86. **Measurement:** the act of finding out the size or amount of something

87. **Mechanism:** the parts or steps that make up a process or activity

88. **Minimum:** as small as possible in amount or degree

89. **Model:** a pattern or figure of something to be made

90. **Modify:** to make changes in something

91. **Molecule**: a group of bonded atoms

92. **Neutrons**: particles with zero charge

93. **Nucleus**: the part of the atom that contains protons and neutrons

94. **Observation:** the act of noting and recording facts and events

95. **Opinion:** a belief based on experience and on seeing certain facts

96. **Optimum:** the best or most favorable degree, condition or amount

97. **Pattern:** a model, guide or plan used in making things

98. **Perform:** to carry out; accomplish

99. **Phenomenon:** an observable fact or event

100. **Potential Energy**: the amount of usable energy a body has when it is at rest

101. **Precision:** the quality of being exactly stated, exact arrangement

102. **Predict:** to figure out and tell beforehand

103. **Preference:** a choosing of or liking for one thing rather than another

104. **Probability:** the quality of being reasonably sure, but not certain, of something happening or being true

105. **Procedure:** the way in which an action or actions are carried out

106. **Proponent:** one who supports a cause

107. **Proportional:** any quantities or measurements having the same fixed relationship

108. **Protons**: particles with a positive energy charge

109. **Radiation**: transfer of energy via rays

110. **Reactants**: substances that are involved in a chemical reaction

111. **Reasonable:** showing or containing sound thought

112. **Refute:** to prove wrong by argument or evidence

113. **Relationship:** the state of being connected

114. **Replicate:** to copy or reproduce

115. **Revise:** to look over again, to correct or improve

116. **Simulation:** the act or process of simulating a system or process

117. **Study:** a careful examination and investigation of an event

118. **Suggest:** to offer as an idea

119. **Summarize:** to state briefly

120. **Support:** to provide evidence

121. **Theory:** a general rule offered to explain experiences or facts

122. **Translate:** to change from one state to another

123. **Treatment:** to expose to some action

124. **Underlying:** to form the support for something

125. **Unit:** a fixed quantity used as a standard of measurement

126. **Validity:** based on evidence that can be supported

127. **Value:** the quantity or amount for which a symbol stands

128. **Variable:** that which can be changed

129. **Viewpoint:** opinion, judgment

130. **Velocity**: the rate of change in distance with respect to time

2. **Familiarize yourself with the entire ACT Science Section and know the three science passage types AND the number of times that each is presented:**

   - Research Summary (three passages)

   - Data Representation (two passages)s

   - Conflicting Viewpoints (one passage)

3. **Know the scoring categories of the Science section:**

   - Interpretation of Data (~45% of total score)

   - Evaluation of Models, Inferences and Experimental Results (~30%)

   - Scientific Investigation (~25% of total score)

4. **Practice working through the three different types of science passages and develop strategies for each type:**

   - **Research Summary**: Three passages of this type include a series of experiments. *Focus on purpose, method and results for each experiment. Students must be able to identify, compare and contrast the differences and similarities between experiments.*

   - **Data Representation**: Two passages of this type will ask you to evaluate data presented in charts, graphs and tables. *Students will want to focus on identifying variables, units and trends.*

   - **Conflicting Viewpoints**: One passage of this type will ask students to compare multiple theories on a single topic presented in narrative passages without diagrams, charts, tables, etc. The ACT is looking for students to identify the purpose, method and results for each experiment. *Students will want to annotate the different scientific evaluations and explanations, highlighting the similarities and differences.*

5. **Take charge of this exam:** Read very, very carefully. Underline or circle detail words to keep track of chart #1 vs. experiment #1 vs. table #1.

6. **Stay in the driver's seat of this exam:** Underline and annotate as you read. These comments will help you as you evaluate and compare results. Note similarities and differences between ideas and experiments.

7. **Understand what you are evaluating:** Ask the following questions:

   - What is this experiment about?
   - What took place in this experiment.
   - Why is the experiment designed this way?
   - What are the dependent and independent variables?
   - Are there patterns or trends?
   - Similarities?
   - Differences?

8. **Only trust the information in the passage:** Do not rely on your working memory of science. Always be able to locate the specific data or reasoning in the passage.

9. **Trust the trends:** Trends will continue outside of the data provided.

10. **Read the questions and ALL of the answers carefully before choosing an answer:** Use an excellent process of elimination, crossing out answers you know are incorrect, starring the "maybe" answers and referring back to the narrative/data for substantiation.

11. **Practice, practice, practice and practice some more:** The more familiar you are with the types of questions, charts, data and opinions presented, the easier it will be for you to answer questions efficiently.

12. **Work on your timing:** You only have six minutes per passage to complete this exam in 35 minutes. Practicing will help you to become faster.

Chapter 10

Math Answers

In this chapter:
• Answers to Algebra Units 1-18 • Answers to Geometry Units 1-4

Algebra Units 1-18 Answers

Sum: the result of addition		
Difference: the result of subtraction		
Product: the result of multiplication		
Quotient: the result of division		
Factors: numbers that form a product		
Digit: a single numeric character (0-9)		
Integers: numbers that have no fractional part (includes negatives, zero, and positives)		
Whole Numbers: positive integers including zero		
Prime Numbers: numbers whose only factors are themselves and one		
Rational Numbers: numbers that can be represented with a fraction		
Real Numbers: number with no complex or imaginary component		
Sequence: an ordered list of numbers		
Arithmetic Sequence: a sequence in which subsequent terms are found by adding or subtracting a constant number		
Geometric Sequence: a sequence in which subsequent terms are found by multiplying or dividing by a constant ratio		

1.	2,367		
2.	3,207		
3.	25,427		
4.	28,079		
5.	920		
6.	538,200		

7.	5,672,249		
8.	1,850,618		
9.	221,125		
10.	507,936		
11.	2,532.44		
12.	64		
13.	0		
14.	Undefined		

PEMDAS:

Parentheses, Exponents, Multiplication, Division, Addition, Subtraction

15.	110		
16.	15		
17.	35		
18.	243		
19.	0		
20.	20		

1.	At 2.25		
2.	e		
3.	30,060,000		
4.	0.0000003006		
5.	32		
6.	59		
7.	$r = P / t$		
8.	14		
9.	77		
10.	16 years old		
11.	3		
12.	-3		
13.	4		
14.	16		
15.	8		
16.	57		
17.	3		
18.	0.56		
19.	2		
20.	4 lbs.		

Unit 3: Polynomials

Variable: a number whose value is unknown or can be changed	
Monomial: a polynomial with only one term	
Binomial: a polynomial with only two terms	
Trinomial: a polynomial with only three terms	
Numerical Coefficient: A constant that multiplies a variable	
Base: the number that is multiplied when using an exponent	
Exponent: the number of times the base should be multiplied - written as a superscript	

1.	$y^2+6y+24$	17.	$16x^3 - 9x^2 y^2 - 6xy$
2.	$4x^2+8$	18.	3
3.	$5x^2-5x+10$	19.	$-q^2 + 3pq + (2/q)$
4.	$2x^2+6y^2+4xy$	20.	$-16x^3+9x^2$
5.	-22		
6.	$-y^5+4y^4+y^2$		
7.	x^2+6x+5		
8.	$3x^2-8x-3$		
9.	$x^2-(x/4)-\frac{1}{8}$		
10.	$x^4-x^3+5x^2-9x-36$		
11.	$6x^4-13x^3-3x^2+29x-20$		
12.	$x^4+4x^3-(19/2)x^2-2x+(9/2)$		
13.	$-6x^5+4x^4+8x^3-6x^2$		
14.	$3x^{11}y^5z^8$		
15.	$3x^3y^4$		
16.	$-3x^3y^5+2xy^3$		

1.	81	22.	x= -3
2.	x= 4	23.	a= 6
3.	5^{20}	24.	$\sqrt[3]{180}$
4.	$\frac{1}{4}x^{12}$	25.	16/9
5.	21^4	26.	$3\text{x}10^6$
6.	$18a^9$	27.	x= 5
7.	$54x^7y^8$	28.	$(7xyz)^2$
8.	x= 2	29.	$6.50\text{x}10^{-8}\ \text{m}^3$
9.	x= 2	30.	31.68 in/min
10.	3.3636 or $\sqrt{8\sqrt{2}}$		
11.	$\dfrac{1}{x^9}$		
12.	$\dfrac{5}{x^4}$		
13.	$\dfrac{1}{(15x)^2}$		
14.	$\left(\dfrac{4}{x}\right)^5$		
15.	$\dfrac{3}{a^3b^8}$		
16.	$\dfrac{a^4b}{7}$		
17.	$\dfrac{3}{a^{17}b^2}$		
18.	$\dfrac{6a^6b^5 - 16 + 9a^7b^6}{-a^5}$		
19.	$\dfrac{y^5}{3x}$		
20.	$10y^7x^{11}$		
21.	x= 3		

$1^2=1$ $2^2=4$ $3^2=9$ $4^2=16$ $5^2=25$ $6^2=36$ $7^2=49$ $8^2=64$			
$9^2=81$ $10^2=100$ $11^2=121$ $12^2=144$ $13^2=169$ $14^2=196$			
$15^2=225$ $16^2=256$ $17^2=289$ $18^2=324$ $19^2=361$ $20^2=400$			
$21^2=441$ $22^2=484$ $23^2=529$ $25^2=625$			
1.	$2\sqrt{10}$	20.	80 volts
2.	$5\sqrt{3}$		
3.	$3\sqrt[3]{6}$		
4.	5		
5.	$\dfrac{1}{64}$		
6.	$3y\sqrt[3]{x}$		
7.	6		
8.	4/5		
9.	4/3		
10.	$\sqrt{5}$		
11.	x= 225		
12.	x= 600		
13.	b= 1284		
14.	x= 4		
15.	x= ⅔ (Take the positive root of the first term and the negative root from the second term)		
16.	b= -8,-3		
17.	2.057s		
18.	12.2 mi		
19.	176.68 or $85 + 41\sqrt{5}$		

1.	30,060,000	26.	$(x-2)(x^2+2x+4)$
2.	99	27.	$8(x-2)(x^2+2x+4)$
3.	$r = P/t$	28.	-640
4.	14	29.	6.25
5.	77	30.	(j)
6.	5.5		
7.	$x= 31/6$		
8.	$y= 1/6$		
9.	$-2\sqrt{6}$		
10.	$16x^6$		
11.	$\dfrac{5x}{6}$		
12.	7		
13.	11		
14.	8		
15.	12		
16.	57		
17.	12		
18.	8		
19.	16		
20.	7		
21.	7/18		
22.	3		
23.	315		
24.	$5*(81)^{4/5}$		
25.	$-x^3-3x^2-50$		

Unit 6: Factoring

1.	7x		
2.	4ab	24.	$(9x^2+7)(x+2)$
3.	$2(x^2-2)$	25.	$(6x^2+1)(3x+5)$
4.	$4p^2q(q^2+6p-4p^2q)$	26.	$(-2x^2-3)(x+2)$
5.	$(x+5)(x-3)$	27.	Det. > 0, two real solutions
6.	$(p+4)(p^2-1)$	28.	Det. > 0, two real solutions
7.	$(x-6)(x+6)$	29.	Det. > 0, two real solutions
8.	$3(5z-7b)(5z+7b)$	30.	Det. < 0, no real solutions
9.	$(x-y-9)(x-y+9)$	31.	L = 12", W = 6" OR L= 6", W = 12"
10.	$(2x-5)(2x+11)$	32.	30 candy bars
11.	$(x-3)(x-5)$	33.	35
12.	$(x+4)(x+8)$	34.	18
13.	$(x-12)(x-4)$	35.	637
14.	$(y+6)(y-3)$	36.	$(x-4)(x^2+4x+16)$
15.	x= -1,-2	37.	x= -5
16.	$(y+6)(y-1)$	38.	7
17.	x= 0,-½, ½	39.	2
18.	$(y+16)^2$	40.	Put the polynomial in standard form Pair the terms: 1st with 2nd, 3rd with 4th Factor the pairs such that what is left is the same for both pairs Condense the remaining terms into factored form.
19.	$(x-2)(x^2+2x+4)$		
20.	$(x+4)(x^2-4x+16)$		
21.	$50(2x-1)(4x^2+2x+1)$		
22.	$3(x+3)(x^2-3x+9)$		
23.	$(10x^2+1)(3x+4)$		

Unit 7: Fractions

1.	4/8	23.	1/120
2.	2/3	24.	$e = \dfrac{a}{1+d}$
3.	13/10	25.	-v
4.	-71/24	26.	125
5.	7/6	27.	31/80
6.	3/8	28.	1/4
7.	8/9	29.	$\dfrac{4x+6}{3x+3} + \dfrac{15x+15}{3x+3}$
8.	4	30.	x= 4/5
9.	5/18		
10.	3/2		
11.	3		
12.	320/27		
13.	$\dfrac{(x+3)(x-1)}{5(x+4)}$		
14.	$\dfrac{2x-1}{4x^2}$		
15.	$\dfrac{7x^2}{49+x}$		
16.	$\dfrac{x-5}{x+5}$		
17.	$\dfrac{4x^2}{(x+1)^2}$		
18.	$\dfrac{(x-7)(x+1)(x-5)}{9(x+5)}$		
19.	2		
20.	148/21		
21.	10/9		
22.	x= -4,-3		

Unit 8: Linear Equations and Lines

1.	-3/2	19.	y= 125x+200 For 5 hours: $825
2.	$y = -\dfrac{3}{2}x - 2$	20.	x=-5, y=6
3.	7/4		
4.	m= ⅔ y-int = -1/3		
5.	b= 2		
6.	y=x+2		
7.	1/7		
8.	$y = -\dfrac{1}{2}x + \dfrac{1}{2}a$		
9.	$y = \dfrac{5}{2}x - 3$		
10.	Matt: 2x+1, Linda: 2x+3 Linda ran 2 more miles than Matt each week.		
11.	MRTB's silo: 10ft tall, Mr. Ross' silo: 15ft tall Mr. Ross' silo is 5ft taller than MRTB's.		
12.	b(0) = -2		
13.	y = 4.715x + 18.65		
14.	y=-14000x+180000		
15.	20 months		
16.	$1,950		
17.	$660		
18.	x < 1: y=0 $x \geq 1: y = 1200(x - 1) + 1500$		

1. m= ¾

$$y = \frac{3}{4}x - \frac{1}{4}$$

x-int= ⅓, y-int= -¼

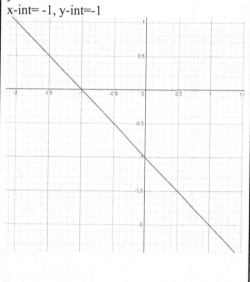

2. m= -1
y=-x-1
x-int= -1, y-int=-1

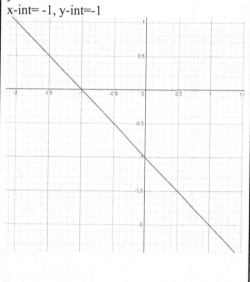

3. Vertex: (1,-4)   AoS: x=1
Min: (1,-4)   Range: $y \geq -4$
Domain: $x \in \Re$

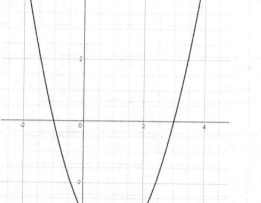

4. Vertex: (1,0)   AoS: x=1
Min: (1,0)   Range: $y \geq 0$
Domain: $x \in \Re$

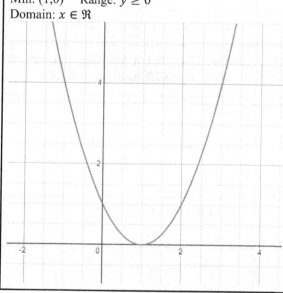

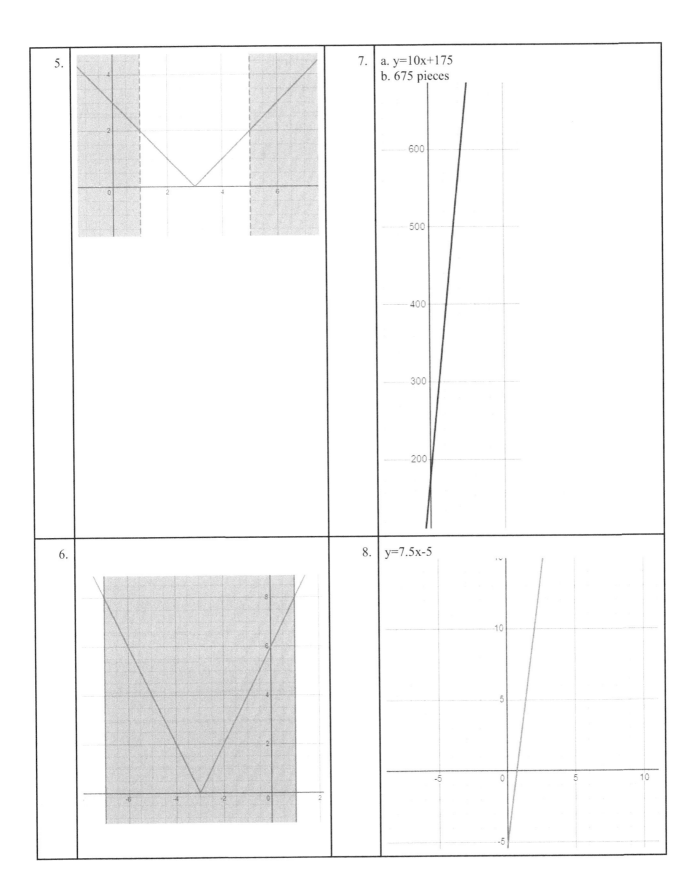

5.

6.

7. a. y=10x+175
    b. 675 pieces

8. y=7.5x-5

9.	$y=5x+65$	19.	Factored: $y=(x-a)(x-b)$ Standard: $y=x^2-(a+b)x+ab$
		20.	1.635
10.	a. $y=-15x+145$ b. c. 8 days		
11.	$20 per bag		
12.	5.89 seconds		
13.	9.618 seconds		
14.	In 2000: 7.8 In 2010: 107.8		
15.	$k=6$		
16.	$c=6.25$		
17.	X-int: -3, -2 Distance: 1		
18.	(4,b)		

1.	Not a solution	13.	Left-handed students: 3 Right-handed students: 27
2.	Not a solution	14.	No solution
3.	x=8, y=-39/13		
4.	x= -2, y= 0		
5.	x=-6/5, y=96/25	15.	Stocks equal at (0.687, 18.437)
6.	x=48, y=34		
7.	 (2, 0)		
8.	No solution 	16.	After 7.812 seconds
		17.	a. b.
9.	-5		
10.	4		
11.	-14		
12.	Online: c=10t+8 At the door: c=12t (4, 48) Intersection point represents the number of tickets where the cost of purchase is the same whether bought online or at the door. Less than 4 tickets, it is less expensive to buy them at the door. More than 4 tickets, it is less expensive to buy them online.		
		18.	13
		19.	11 120-pound packages
		20.	3/2

21.	Two possible solutions: $(a,b) = (7,144), (30,121)$		

1.	$\dfrac{2de}{e-d}$	12.	y=-6x-37 X-int: -37/6, Y-int: -37 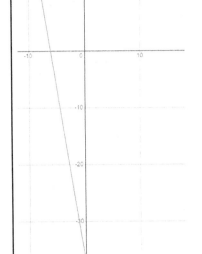
2.	1/6		
3.	5x³-22x²-3x-53		
4.	$(x+7)+\dfrac{22x+20}{(x+1)(x-2)}$		
5.	x= 2, y= -1		
6.	After buying 24 CD's		
7.	After using 15.17GB of data		
8.	Solutions: (0.725, 4.175), (8.275, 26.825) 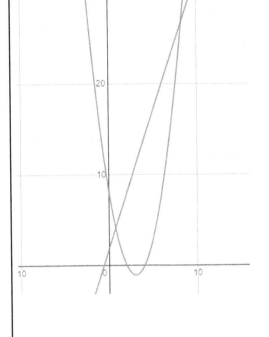	13.	y=x X-int: 0, Y-int: 0 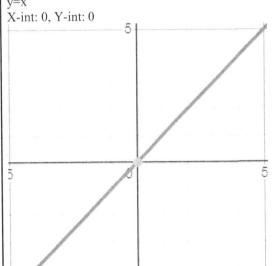
9.	Never		
10.	$y \geq \dfrac{1}{3}x - 2$		
11.	$29,166 per year		

14.	$y = -2\|x + 3\| + 3$ Stretch: -2 X-int: -4.5, -1.5 Y-int: -3 		
15.	a= -6		
16.	4		
17.	(-0.5, -1)		
18.	9074.4		
19.	1		
20.	f(x) = (x+5)²-6		

1.	1/11	24.	25%
2.	2/3	25.	40
3.	13/40	26.	20 hours
4.	1/3	27.	$65.8
5.	39.57 miles per gallon	28.	2,647,753.38 are recycled daily 12,061,987.62 are not recycled
6.	$14 per ticket	29.	20% more
7.	4.5 inches per hour	30.	$753.42
8.	$670 per person		
9.	21		
10.	1		
11.	8/5		
12.	2.1		
13.	31%		
14.	37.5%		
15.	120%		
16.	233%		
17.	24		
18.	24		
19.	6		
20.	40%		
21.	12.5%		
22.	6.25%		
23.	140		

1.	Domain: (1,-2,0,-1,2) Range: (5,8,4,5,8)	23.	-6
2.	Yes, because for each x-value there is only one y-value.	24.	3
3.	Domain: (4,7,3,4) Range: (1,2,-2,0,-1)	25.	5
4.	No, because there are two y-values at x=7.		
5.	-8		
6.	-137		
7.	3x-5		
8.	x-3		
9.	-x-1		
10.	3x-4		
11.	$2x^2-6x+4$		
12.	$\dfrac{2x-4}{x-1}$		
13.	2x-6		
14.	2x-5		
15.	$y = \dfrac{x-22}{11}$		
16.	y=2x+10		
17.	$y = \sqrt{x+1}$		
18.	$y = \dfrac{-2x+6}{x-15}$		
19.	1		
20.	78		
21.	18		
22.	384×10^4 people		

1.	$4317.85		
2.	$4416.08		
3.	$4439.28		
4.	$4450.69		
5.	$4451.08		
6.	$1,842,165.72		
7.	$,1940,642.39		
8.	$1,964,192.39		
9.	$197,5815.26		
10.	$1,976,213.12		
11.	$20,800		
12.	$112,362.00		
13.	$93,086.00		
14.	$73,810.00		
15.	$3600		
16.	(d)		
17.	B=1500*(1+0.2*t)		
18.	a= 1.54		
19.	$0.0987 per hour		
20.	821.54 grams		

1.	$12i\sqrt{x}$	24.	$\dfrac{7-26i}{25}$
2.	$i\sqrt{254}$	25.	39-80i
3.	a-bi	26.	x= i
4.	5+6i	27.	7-i
5.	11+3i	28.	-60-24i
6.	-2+7i	29.	$x = -1 \pm 3i$
7.	$i\sqrt{35}$	30.	$\dfrac{-5}{6} \pm \dfrac{\sqrt{11}}{6}i$
8.	9i		
9.	-1		
10.	-i		
11.	35i		
12.	7		
13.	3i		
14.	-12		
15.	6		
16.	$\dfrac{-12i\sqrt{7}}{7}$		
17.	$i/4$		
18.	-24i		
19.	-15		
20.	$\dfrac{30+5i}{37}$		
21.	$x^2 + x(3-2i) - 6i$		
22.	x-9i		
23.	$\dfrac{x+6i}{x^2+36}$		

Mean/Average: a metric used to perceive the center of a dataset - susceptible to bias due to outliers
Mode: the most common value in a dataset
Median: the center value when the dataset is sorted by value - not affected by outliers
Range: the distance between the lowest and highest values in a dataset
Interquartile Range: the difference between the 25% quartile and 75% quartile values - 50% of the data points are within this range
Scatter Plot: a graph where data is shown as separate points
Correlation: when two variables appear to be related
Probability: the chance of something occurring
Basic Probability: probability based on random chance
Conditional Probability: the probability of something given prior knowledge of something else
Independent Probability: when probability is not influenced by previous events
Dependent Probability: when probability is influenced by previous events
Fundamental Counting Principle: a method to determine the number of possible outcomes based on stages and the alternatives within each stage

1.	Mean: 157.8 Mode: None Median: 155		
2.	Mean: 45.86 Mode: 25 Median: 36		
3.	11/2		
4.	x-1		
5.	4/3		

6.	22		
7.	86		
8.	91	22.	a. Positive
9.	15	23.	b. Negative
10.	10	24.	c. none Range: 4 IQR: 2 0.00148
11.	9	25.	2/5
12.	1/20	26.	Dependent, because the probability of choosing the second person was increased by choosing the first person.
13.	2/5	27.	Independent
14.	65.7%	28.	Dependent, because plates that have already been made cannot be reused.
15.	1/21	29.	Independent
16.	11 green marbles	30.	18 different sundaes
17.	0.719		
18.	0.0126		
19.	0.04		
20.	5040 configurations		
21.	640 applicants		

1.	x= 2z - 6		
2.	89.2		
3.	80%		
4.	80 men		
5.	2400 eggs		
6.	20 pairs of jeans		
7.	$y = -\dfrac{3}{2}x + \dfrac{3}{2}$		
8.	-i		
9.	a. $337,209.30 b. $453,125.00 c. $690,476.19		
10.	36 hours		
11.	a. $2x^3+7x^2+11x+4$ b. X^2-x+5 c. $-x^2+5x-3$		
12.	$\dfrac{6}{13} - \dfrac{5}{26}i$		
13.	$f(g(x)) = -2x^2 + 14$ $g(f(x)) = -4x^2 - 16x - 11$		
14.	$\dfrac{i}{2}$		
15.	f(2) = 22, f(-5) = 52		
16.	$49.42		
17.	2		
18.	248,623,402.57		
19.	a= 5		
20.	No, the highest grade Georgia can earn is 85.49		

Data: a collection of information about a topic
Population: a group studied for statistical purposes
Sample: a subcomponent of a population from which data is collected - should be representative of the larger population
Integrity of Sample: how well the sample represents the larger population
Variance: a measure of how data points differ from the mean - the square of standard deviation
Standard Deviation: a measure of how dense a dataset is
Normal Distribution: the bell-shaped gaussian curve that often accurately models real-world data
Permutation: a configuration or sequence in which order and value matters
Combination: a configuration or sequence in which only the values matter
Factorial: a mathematical operation where the argument is multiplied by every integer between it and zero

1.	Yes		
2.	No		
3.	10		
4.	126		
5.	No, because the sample is not random.		
6.	Median		
7.	10 piles		
8.	1,860,480 different standings		
9.	120		
10.	252		

1.	1/2	17.	$cos\theta = \dfrac{\sqrt{8}}{3}$ $tan\theta = \dfrac{1}{\sqrt{8}}$
2.	$\dfrac{\sqrt{3}}{2}$		
3.	$\dfrac{1}{\sqrt{3}}$		
4.	$\dfrac{\sqrt{3}}{2}$	18.	$cos\theta = \dfrac{5}{\sqrt{26}}$ $sin\theta = \dfrac{1}{\sqrt{26}}$
5.	1/2		
6.	$\sqrt{3}$		
7.	$\dfrac{\sqrt{2}}{2}$	19.	5/13
8.	$\dfrac{\sqrt{2}}{2}$	20.	$\sqrt{1-a^2}$
9.	1	21.	Undefined.
10.	4/5	22.	0.629
11.	3/5	23.	a. $\frac{6}{\sqrt{61}}$
12.	4/3		b. $\frac{5}{\sqrt{61}}$
13.	3/5		c. 6/5
14.	4/5		d. $\frac{\sqrt{61}}{6}$
15.	3/4		e. $\frac{\sqrt{61}}{5}$
			f. 5/6

16.	$cos\theta = \frac{\sqrt{3}}{2}$ $tan\theta = \frac{1}{\sqrt{3}}$ 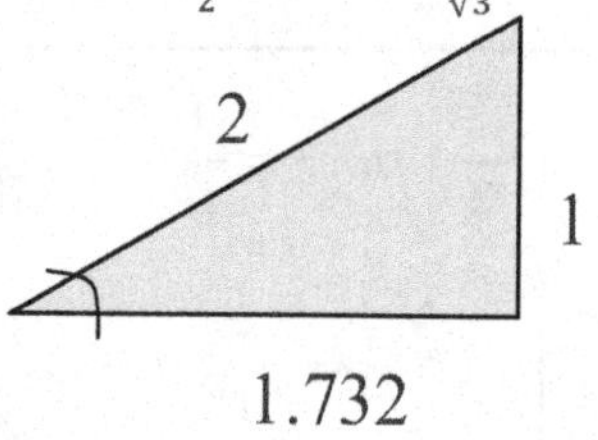	24.	5/13
		25.	$\frac{\sqrt{29}}{2}$
		26.	3/5
		27.	Sides: 10 Hypotenuse: 14.14
		28.	a
		29.	AB = 20 AC=$10\sqrt{3}$
		30.	(3,4,5); (5,12,13); (7,24,25)

1.		6.	
2.		7.	4
		8.	$\dfrac{\pi}{4}$
3.		9.	24 radians right
		10.	6 up
		11.	$x \in \Re$
		12.	Range: [2,10]
		13.	$\sin^2\theta, + \cos^2\theta = 1$
4.		14.	1
5.		15.	

Geometry Answers: Units 1-4

1.	a. 138° b. 42° c. 42° d. 138° e. 138° f. 42° g. 42° h. 138°	5.	120°
		6.	76°
		7.	59°
		8.	149°
		9.	59.7°
2.	a. Y° b. 180° - Y° c. 180° - Y° d. Y°	10.	45°
3.	a. 110° b. 70° c. 70° d. 110° e. 110° f. 70° g. 70° h. 110°		
4.	a. 140° b. 40° c. 40° d. 140° e. 155° f. 25° g. 25° h. 155°		

Unit 2: Triangles

1.	55° Scalene, Acute	15.	3
2.	95° Scalene, Obtuse	16.	A=B= 45° X=Y= 9.9
3.	A= 40° B= 140° X= 140° Y= 40° Z= 100° Isosceles, Obtuse	17.	X= 3 Y= 4.24 A=B= 45° Area= 4.5
		18.	247.43 in²
4.	a. 45° b. 55° Scalene, Acute	19.	A: B = 5:12
		20.	200
5.	a. 15° b. 100° c. 80° d. 65° e. 40° f. 83° g. 123° h. 57° i. 83° j. 70° k. 70°		
6.	24, Scalene, Acute		
7.	a. Right b. Congruent SAS		
8.	Isosceles, Similar		
9.	11		
10.	79°		
11.	27.7°		
12.	3.9		
13.	4 in		
14.	110.85 in²		

1.	a. 180° b. 360° c. 360° d. 540° e. 720° f. 900° g. 1080° h. 1260° i. 1440°		
2.	150°		
3.	78°		
4.	142°, 38°, 142°		
5.	Diagonals: 33.9 ft Perimeter: 88 ft Area: 576 ft²		
6.	Minimum of 6		
7.	38.97		
8.	120°		
9.	60°		
10.	Area = 52 Perimeter = 36		
11.	4 cm		
12.	AC = 4.24 DE = 2.12		
13.	a. 110° b. 180° c. 110° d. 35°		
14.	18.14		
15.	100		

Unit 4: Circles

#		#	
1.	a. BE, CG, DF b. BE, DF c. BA, AE, FA, AD d. CG e. 10 f. 25.13 g. 113.097	15.	9 in
2.	a. 22.21 in b. 39.27 in^2		
3.	a. 28.27 ft^2 b. 36.0 ft^2		
4.	a. 50.27 ft^2 b. 16.0 ft^2 c. 19.31 ft d. 34.27 ft^2		
5.	a. 3.14159 cm b. 9.42 cm c. 3.14159 cm d. 9.42 cm e. 18.84 cm		
6.	a. 12.83 cm^2 b. 64.14 cm^2 c. 12.83 cm^2		
7.	Largest: 90° Smallest: 25°		
8.	a. Circumference increases by a factor of 3. b. Area increases by a factor of 9.		
9.	18.85 in^2		
10.	2.625 in		
11.	176.71 ft^2		
12.	42.41 in^3		
13.	12.57 ft^3 or 21,714.7 in^3		
14.	a. 10,560 ft b. 1,344.54 revolutions		

Notes

In this chapter:
• Space for Notes on Class Lectures
• Space for Notes on College Visits
• Space for Notes on College Essays
• Space for your To-Do List

Made in the USA
Columbia, SC
22 August 2024